REINCARNATION
IN THE
BIBLE?

REINCARNATION
IN THE
BIBLE?

Dan Carlton

authorHOUSE®

AuthorHouse™ LLC
1663 Liberty Drive
Bloomington, IN 47403
www.authorhouse.com
Phone: 1-800-839-8640

Published by AuthorHouse   04/03/2014

ISBN: 978-1-4918-1100-9 (sc)
ISBN: 978-1-4918-1099-6 (e)

Unless otherwise indicated, all Scripture quotations are taken from the King James Version of the Bible.

Scripture quotations marked NIV are taken from the HOLY BIBLE, NEW INTERNATIONAL VERSION. Copyright © 1973, 1978, 1984 International Bible Society. Used by permission of Zondervan Bible Publishers.

Scripture quotations marked NASB are taken from the New American Standard Bible, © 1960, 1962, 1963, 1968, 1971, 1972, 1973, 1975, 1977, by The Lockman Foundation. Used by permission.

CONTENTS

DEDICATION

My primary dedication is to God who created everything and everyone. Second, my mother and father without whose cooperation I would not be here. Without their guidance, instruction and example, which I rebelled against most of my life, I may not have asked the questions and sought the answers that led me to the conclusions I am sharing in this book.

My mother, Dr. Edith Lord, had the greatest influence on me during my younger years, although her parents and brothers and sisters also played a part. While she was going to college she supplemented her income by teaching English and at home she never missed an opportunity to correct mine, which has been helpful in my attempt to communicate. Until she passed on at the age of 81, she continued to exert a positive influence on me for which I am grateful.

I didn't see much of my Father, but he and my stepmother, Mable, did play a part in raising me, along with others on my Father's side of the family such as my Grandfather who was a medical doctor and my Grandmother. Also, there was my Uncle Bob and Aunt Jane who took me in for a year in Salt Lake City, Utah while my mother was recovering from an illness.

The Holy Bible and many scholars and commentators on Scripture also influenced me including Edgar Cayce and Garner Ted Armstrong. The more I think about those who influenced me in my lifetime search for the truth, the longer the list grows. I would have to include my wife, Carolyn, my children, Mike, Brenda, Tom, Beth and my friend, Margie who all played a part by refusing to accept some of my conclusions and therefore spurring me to rethink those conclusions and either modify or confirm them. The list grows too long. There are many who influenced me in ways I would consider negative and yet even those can result in a positive outcome in the long run. Every experience teaches us something and tends to point us in a direction. Fortunately we have God's written revelation of absolute truth to keep us on the right road if we will read and heed His directions. In the final analysis He must be our primary influence; the light of the world; the way, the truth and the life.

INTRODUCTION

Who in the world is Dan Carlton? I have wondered about that all my life, which began September 3, 1929 in Escanaba, Michigan. A month later the stock market crashed and the whole world went into a deep depression, which I hope wasn't caused by my sudden appearance on the scene.

Primarily my mother raised me and sometimes farmed me out to her parents while she continued her education. Her father and mother had six children and thought I would be better off if I was adopted by them and raised to think they were my parents instead of my grandparents. My mother disagreed but my grandparents hoped she would eventually change her mind so while I was living with them they taught me to call them Mom and Dad. After several months had passed my mother came by for a visit and was shocked when I called her Edith instead of Mother. She took me for a long drive and explained very carefully that she was my mother. Finally I looked at her very soberly and said, "Well, you may be my mother but you still look like Edith to me!"

Since I don't have any letters after my name (except "L"—Layman) I cannot brag about my authority as a highly educated scholar. I believe I have an average I.Q. and I can read and reason things out (although I'll have to admit, not everyone agrees with me about that!). I don't claim any special abilities that aren't possessed by every normal person. My formal education ended in the tenth grade but I have a high school diploma by virtue of a G.E.D. test I took in the military. I tried college but dropped out after a year because I really didn't have a clear idea of what I wanted to do with my life.

When I was a child I wondered about such things as where we come from, why are we here, where do we go after death, is there a creator God and if so does He reveal Himself to us, and if so how? Is the Bible really His inspired revelation to us? Is evolution true as an alternative to creation or did God create evolution and then leave it to run its course?

I was taught by my relatives and society that evolution is true and the Bible is merely the result of ignorant men trying to explain things they did not understand and is therefore filled with superstitions, distorted history, exaggerations and other false information. My family was primarily agnostic although they did suspect that there is a God out there somewhere but whenever they attempted to describe Him it sounded like they were making up a god they could control.

I have shared my conclusions with others including church members, preachers, scholars and unbelievers and have discovered no one agrees with me. Not only do they all disagree with me but they also disagree with each other as well as the Bible—in my humble opinion. So I have incorporated what I believe agrees with science and Scripture and rejected the rest. But even though I believe what I believe is true I also believe I could be wrong and I continue to seek and study.

In my early twenties I read a book that started me in a completely different direction. Up to that time I had been taught to be agnostic and believed the Bible to be the result of ignorant men trying to explain what they did not understand with superstition, fables, exaggerated history, etc. The book is *There is a River* by Thomas Sugrue. It is a biography of the best-documented clairvoyant in history—Edgar Cayce. When he was in a trance he was able to "see" into a person's body and accurately reveal his physical condition. Then he could prescribe therapy to heal the person. If followed, the therapy always worked. Often, while in trance, he would use technical medical terms he did not understand when he woke up. His formal education did not go beyond the eighth grade. One example of his ability is the story of a woman who had taken her daughter to several doctors with an illness they all agreed could not be cured, and of which she would shortly die. The mother heard about Cayce and came to him as a last resort.

He went into his trance and told the mother to give her daughter a dose of belladonna. Cayce had a doctor friend he consulted with for fear he might prescribe something that would harm someone. When asked, his friend said the dose of belladonna was enough to kill several men. Other doctors agreed, so Cayce told the mother what he had learned. She decided to go ahead with the therapy, reasoning that her daughter would die anyway and so far Cayce's therapies had always worked. After giving her daughter the belladonna, she was to wait a specific length of time, and then give her something to make her vomit. She applied the therapy and her daughter recovered and was still alive as an adult at the time the book was written.

After several thousand successful "readings," as they were called, Cayce was asked in trance where we come from, why are we here, and where do we go after death. His answers included the assertion that the Bible is the Word of God and everything in it is accurate. He also claimed reincarnation is a fact. After reading this, I started studying the Bible and have continued this study to the present. I have examined commentaries from many scholars and after comparing their conclusions with Scripture, I have adopted what I believe agrees with Scripture and rejected the rest. I have discovered they all agree with Scripture most of the time, but not all the time, in my humble opinion. Perhaps I am a reincarnated Berean (Acts 17:10,11). I have continued to keep an open mind, believing my conclusions are correct but also realizing I could be wrong.

I have discussed my conclusions with others, trying to find where I might be wrong. Usually people get mad at me when they find out I don't believe the way they do. I have been invited to stay away from some churches after they discovered my belief didn't match theirs and they were unable to persuade me that I disagree with Scripture. Perhaps they are right, and I am either too hardheaded, or too stupid to realize it. Or perhaps I am right and they are wrong. I noticed those different churches not only disagreed with me but also with themselves. They can't all be right, can they? But they could all be wrong, couldn't they? I have written to several scholars explaining what I believe and why and they have all disagreed with me. They also seemed to disagree with Scripture as well as themselves.

My main focus has been the doctrine of salvation. I believe this is the most important doctrine in the Bible. If we have salvation right and we are wrong about everything else, we will still receive eternal life and vice versa. A few years ago I started writing down my conclusions in order to clarify to myself just what I did believe. I could not accept the idea that I could be right when everyone I talked to disagreed with me. And yet my conclusions do seem to me to agree with Scripture, including my belief in reincarnation, which I believe is not only a fact revealed in the Bible but is a necessary part of God's plan of salvation. After awhile I realized I had written a book and I thought that if possible I would share my understanding of God's plan of salvation with a larger number of people, hoping that if I am wrong, someone will be able to show me where. On the other hand, if I'm right, perhaps more people will join me on the narrow road to eternal life. Another motivating factor in my desire to share my understanding of truth is my belief that all of the problems in the world can be traced to erroneous belief. I believe if everyone correctly understood and applied truth, our problems would vanish. God says we become what we think (Pr. 23:7). My belief that the Bible teaches that reincarnation is a fact hasn't endeared me to those who not only reject such an idea but also sincerely believe such a belief comes from the pit of hell and smells of smoke. After reading "Reincarnation in the Bible?" perhaps you can show me where I am in error, if you disagree with me. Or who knows, perhaps you will agree with me. At any rate I hope you find my book interesting and enjoyable, if not enlightening.

CHAPTER ONE

BEGINNINGS

Join me on an imaginary trip into the past—way back into the past. Let's go all the way back to the very beginning of the universe. There are some who believe the universe had no beginning; that it has always existed. I think most scientists disagree with such a belief. One reason they give is the existence of radioactivity. Radioactive materials still exist and are still in the process of breaking down into stable materials. The stars are a good example of this process. There are still stars burning with what scientists call thermonuclear fusion, including our sun. The universe cannot be infinitely old or all useable energy would have been lost already (entropy). This has not occurred. Therefore, the universe is not infinitely old. If the universe has always existed, everything would be in equilibrium. The whole universe would be stable. There would be no movement and no difference in temperature. Since that is not the state of the universe, it must have had a beginning. So imagine we are standing at the very beginning of the universe. Since it did have a beginning, then there must have been a time before the beginning. Now let's take another step into the past. Let's go back before the beginning. What will we be likely to find here? Well we should expect to find nothing shouldn't we? Absolutely nothing! Not even a single atom. Not even a single electron. Nothing! In every direction from where we are standing there is nothing but totally empty space.

But what is space? Where did it come from? Where does it begin? Where does it end? But how is this possible? How can it extend in all directions from our imaginary position without ending? It cannot end, can it? What would lie on the other side of the end? On the other hand, how can it not end? These seem to be the only two possibilities and yet neither of them is possible, are they? Using logic and experience, we have arrived at a point that we are unable to understand or explain.

As if that were not enough of a problem, consider the fact that out of this absolute nothingness the universe appears. But how is that possible? All of our experience and logic tell us something cannot come from nothing by any natural source. And yet there it is. Sane people cannot deny that the universe does exist, can they? Using our experience and logic, we would have to conclude that the existence of the universe is impossible, and yet it does exist.

Have you ever thought about these things? Would you agree with me that we cannot answer these questions using observation, experience, experimentation, and logic? These questions seem to be beyond our ability to answer. If there is an answer, I've never heard one that is based on observation, experience, experimentation, facts and logic. We will have to admit that there are some facts that we simply do not have the ability to understand or explain.

Jesus has always existed

The only way we have of understanding some things that we cannot understand using observation, experience, experimentation, and logic, is to have these things revealed to us by someone who does know the answers. God is the only person I know who fits that description and in His written revelation to mankind we can find the answers to everything He wants us to know at this time. I believe He has revealed that before the beginning of everything He existed. He had no beginning and will have no end. He is eternal. He exists in three persons: God the Father, God the Son, and God the Holy Spirit. In John 3:16 we are told that Jesus is God's only begotten son, which would indicate that He had a beginning rather than existing from eternity past like God the Father. One scripture that clearly says Jesus has always existed is Micah 5:2: "But thou,

Bethlehem Ephratah, *though* thou be little among the thousands of Judah, *yet* out of thee shall he come forth unto me *that is* to be ruler in Israel; whose goings forth *have been* from of old, from everlasting." The word translated "everlasting" from the Hebrew literally means "the days of eternity." Other scriptures indicating that Jesus has existed from eternity past like the Father are:

> ➤ "Blessed be the LORD God of Israel from everlasting, to everlasting" (Ps. 41:13; 106:48).

> ➤ "Thy throne is established of old, Thou art from everlasting" (Ps. 93:2).

> ➤ "Art thou not from everlasting, O LORD my God, mine Holy One?" (Hab. 1:12).

It can be argued that these scriptures refer to God the Father, not the Son. This is what I used to believe until I discovered that Jesus is the God of the Old Testament.

Jesus is Yahweh

When God spoke to Moses from the burning bush, Moses asked Him His name. "And God said unto Moses, I AM THAT I AM. And He said, Thus shalt thou say unto the children of Israel, I AM hath sent me unto you" (Ex. 3:14). Jesus referred to Himself more than once as "I AM":

> "Then spake Jesus again unto them saying, **I am** the light of the world. He that followeth Me shall not walk in darkness, but shall have the light of life...I said therefore unto you, that ye shall die in your sins, for if ye believe not that **I am** *He*, ye shall die in your sins... Then said Jesus unto them, When ye have lifted up the Son of man, then shall ye know that **I am** *He*, and that I do nothing of Myself, but as My Father hath taught Me, I speak these things...Jesus said unto them, Verily, verily, I say unto you, before Abraham was, **I am**" (John 8:12,24,28,58).

In these verses notice the word *"He"* is in italics. The King James translators added connecting words at times so the English version of the Bible would flow more smoothly. They put these words in italics so the reader would understand that those words were not in the Greek manuscripts from which they were translating. In the Greek manuscripts the word *"He"* was missing. So Jesus was saying, "I am," not "I am He." In these verses and others, Jesus was saying He was the same God who spoke to Moses out of the burning bush. In verse 28 above, we can also learn something else that many miss. In this verse He says; "…**I am**, and that I do nothing of Myself, but as My Father hath taught Me, I speak these things." Jesus is saying that He is not the Father, isn't He? Since He claims He is the God who spoke to Moses out of the burning bush, and that God's personal name was YHWH, or Yahweh, then Yahweh is not God the Father but rather God the Son.

Jesus—just a good man?

During Jesus' condemnation of the hypocritical scribes and Pharisees, He made this statement:

> "Wherefore, behold, I send unto you prophets, and wise men, and scribes: and *some* of them ye shall kill and crucify; and *some* of them shall ye scourge in your synagogues, and persecute *them* from city to city" (Mt. 23:34).

Could He have made that statement if He were just a "good" man? Since it would be a false statement it would disqualify Him from the title "good," wouldn't it? On the other hand, He could honestly make that statement only if He were God.

It is hard for me understand how anyone can praise Jesus if they do not believe He is God. If He was just a man, then what about the claims He made such as:

> ➤ "The Son of man shall send forth his angels, and they shall gather out of his kingdom all things that offend, and them which do iniquity; And shall cast them into a furnace of fire: there shall be wailing and gnashing of teeth." (Mt. 13:41,42).

> ➤ "For the Son of man shall come in the glory of his Father with his angels; and then he shall reward every man according to his works." (Mt. 16:27).

> ➤ "The Son of man shall be betrayed into the hands of men: And they shall kill him, and the third day he shall be raised again" (Mt 17:22,23).

> ➤ "I am the way, the truth, and the life: no man cometh unto the Father, but by me." (Jhn 14:6).

If a man said these things, He was the most evil fraud in history since millions of His followers were tortured and killed (and still are at the hands of Muslims and other godless people around the world). If His followers were lying why did they willingly face torture and death to spread those lies? Also, remember that Jesus walked on water, raised the dead, healed the sick, blind, crippled and accepted worship, even though He reminded Satan only God could accept worship: "And saith unto him, All these things will I give thee, if thou wilt fall down and worship me. Then saith Jesus unto him, Get thee hence, Satan: for it is written, Thou shalt worship the Lord thy God, and him only shalt thou serve" (Mt. 4:9,10). Finally He was killed, buried, rose from the grave and ascended to heaven. And we are to believe this was just a man and not God?

All the historical events recorded in the New Testament were written within the lifetime of eyewitnesses. Had anything been incorrect, it would have been corrected, especially by Christ's enemies. There was no time for the alleged fables to arise. There is more textual evidence for the events in the New Testament than any figure of ancient history. If you believe in the reality of Buddha, Mohammad, Plato or any figure in ancient history, you logically have to believe in the reality of Christ and the people and events recorded.

"I'm trying, here, to prevent anyone saying the really foolish thing that people often say about him. 'I am ready to accept Jesus as a great moral teacher, but I don't accept his claim to be God.' That is the one thing we must not say. A man who is merely a man and said the sorts of things Jesus said would not be a great moral teacher; he would either be a lunatic on the level with a man who says he is a poached egg, or else he would be the devil of hell. You must make your choice. Either this man was and is the Son of God, or else a madman or something worse. You can shut him up for a fool, you can spit at him and kill him as a demon, or you can fall at his feet and call him Lord and God. But let us not come up with any patronizing nonsense about his being a great human teacher. He has not left that open to us. He did not intend to" (C. S. Lewis).

One of the best passages in the Bible proving Jesus is Yahweh is found in Zechariah 12. It begins in verse one with Yahweh saying; "The burden of the word of the LORD for Israel, saith the LORD, which stretcheth forth the heavens, and layeth the foundation of the earth, and formeth the spirit of man within him." He continues to speak in the first person all the way to verse ten, where He, Yahweh, says; "And I will pour upon the house of David, and upon the inhabitants of Jerusalem, the spirit of grace and of supplications: and they shall look upon me whom they have pierced…" The only person who could possibly be referred to here as the one "whom they have pierced," is Jesus. Surely we can agree that God the Father is not the one who was pierced, can't we? After this point, Yahweh begins speaking in the third person in the last half of the same verse; "…and they shall mourn for him, as one mourneth for *his* only *son*, and shall be in bitterness for him, as one that is in bitterness for *his* firstborn." Jesus, as Yahweh, may be referring to Himself in the third person to describe the reaction of His disciples at His crucifixion. We see numerous examples in both the old and new testaments where God/Jesus speaks of Himself in the third person.

The Word

John starts his Gospel by saying: "In the beginning was the Word, and the Word was with God, and the Word was God. The same was in the beginning with God. All things were made by Him, and without Him was not any thing made that was made." (John 1:1-3). Paul states: "Who is the image of the invisible God, the firstborn of every creature. For by Him were all things created that are in heaven and that are in earth, visible and invisible, whether they be thrones or dominions or principalities or powers, all things were created by Him and for Him, and He is before all things, and by Him all things consist" (Col. 1:15-17). These verses seem to be revealing that Jesus is the same God of Genesis 1:1: "In the beginning God created the heaven and the earth." There are some who believe the phrase "firstborn of every creature" means Jesus was the first to be created by God. Paul uses the Greek word *prototokos,* which means first in rank, preeminent one, rather than *protoktisis,* which does mean first created. That word is never used of Jesus. It is showing that Christ has the same privileges and rights in His creation as the human firstborn had in his family. After all, John begins his Gospel declaring Jesus is God, so He cannot be created, can He? In Hebrews we learn:

> "Hath in these last days spoken unto us by His Son whom He hath appointed heir of all things, by whom also He made the worlds, who being the brightness of His glory and the express image of His person, and upholding all things by the word of His power, when He had by Himself purged our sins, sat down on the right hand of the Majesty on high . . . But unto the Son He saith, Thy throne, O God, is for ever and ever, a sceptre of righteousness is the sceptre of Thy Kingdom" (Heb. 1:2,3,8).

Here God is calling Jesus God.

Isaiah prophesied: "For unto us a child is born, unto us a Son is given and the government shall be on His shoulder and He will

be called Wonderful, Counselor, The Mighty God, The Everlasting
Father, The Prince of Peace" (Isa. 9:6).

The first and the last

In Isaiah 44:6, God is speaking in the first person: "Thus says
the LORD the King of Israel, and His redeemer the LORD of hosts;
I am the first and I am the last and beside Me there is no God." In
Revelation Jesus is speaking in the first person:

> "I am Alpha and Omega, the first and the last . . .
> Fear not, I am the first and the last . . . These things says
> the first and the last, which was dead, and is alive . . .
> I am Alpha and Omega, the beginning and the end, the
> first and the last" (Rev. 1:11; 1:17; 2:8; 22:13).

Since there can only be one "first and last," then it seems to
me that the inescapable conclusion has to be that Jesus and Yahweh
(the God of the Old Testament) are one and the same person.

YHWH

Also notice in Isaiah 44:6 above, the word LORD in all capitals
is the way the translators chose to indicate the special personal
name of God written in the Hebrew as YHWH. Scholars agree that
no one knows for sure how that name should be pronounced but
most scholars agree it should be pronounced Yahweh. Notice in
this verse it is used twice, indicating two separate individuals. If we
translate the verse using Yahweh in place of LORD, it reads: "Thus
saith [Yahweh] the King of Israel, and His redeemer [Yahweh] of
hosts..." This seems a little confusing, doesn't it? Perhaps we are
getting a glimpse here of the unity of the Holy Trinity. Jesus, as
Yahweh of the Old Testament, is referring to Himself as redeemer
in the New Testament. Yahweh is His Old Covenant name. He is
known as Jesus in the New Covenant.

Only one savior

In the Old Testament, Yahweh says; "I, even I, am the LORD and beside Me there is no saviour" (Isa. 43:11). In the New Testament the Holy Spirit inspires Peter to say; "Neither is there salvation in any other, for there is none other name under heaven given among men whereby we must be saved" (Acts 4:12). So we find Yahweh saying He is the only savior, and Jesus through the Holy Spirit, saying He is the only savior. One of these statements is false unless Jesus and Yahweh are the same God.

Christ created everything

Paul was inspired to write: ". . . Jesus Christ, by whom are all things . . ." (1 Cor. 8:6). In Hebrews 1:1,2 we are told: "God . . . hath in these last days spoken unto us by His Son, whom He hath appointed heir of all things, by whom also He made the worlds." Clearly Christ is the God referred to in Genesis 1:1. Christ is the God who created everything and everyone. Christ is the God of the Old Testament.

Glory

Many believe Yahweh is the personal name of God the Father. One reason I believe that is an error—in addition to the above scriptures—is because in Isaiah 42:8 Yahweh says, "I am the LORD, that is My name, and My glory will I not give to another." He repeats this statement in Isaiah 48:11. In John 17:5, Jesus is praying:

> "And now, O Father, glorify Thou Me with Thine
> own self, with the glory which I had with Thee before
> the world was."

If Yahweh is God the Father, either He or Jesus made a false statement. Yahweh said He would never share His glory with another and Jesus said He had glory with the Father before the world was created. One of these statements is false unless Jesus and Yahweh are the same person and Yahweh is not the Father.

Does begotten mean Jesus had a beginning?

So what about that word "begotten"? John could not mean that Jesus had a beginning, because he begins his gospel declaring that Jesus is God. Also, he is quoting Jesus. In the Greek, begotten means unique or one of a kind. Jesus has the same divine nature as the Father. When He claimed to be the Son of God, the authorities tried to kill Him: "Therefore the Jews sought the more to kill him, because he not only had broken the sabbath, but said also that God was his Father, making himself equal with God" (John 5:18). Another possibility is this is referring to Christ's incarnation in the flesh. Jesus was begotten of the Holy Spirit from the Father through Mary (Mt. 1:18). Christ is one with the Father and the Holy Spirit. In the prophecy of Christ's coming, which I mentioned above, we are told, "Thou art My Son, this day have I begotten Thee" (Ps. 2:7). Paul refers to this prophecy in Acts 13:33 while speaking in Antioch. It is referred to again in Hebrews 1:5 and 5:5. Christ was the Father's only begotten Son in the flesh, and later became the first begotten of the dead (Rev. 1:5).

Trinity

Many people reject God's truth as revealed in the Word of God. Thank God His truth does not depend on our acceptance. His truth is always true regardless of what we choose to believe. The first reference to the trinity is found in Genesis 1:26,27:

> "And God said, Let us make man in our image, after
> our likeness: and let them have dominion over the fish of
> the sea, and over the fowl of the air, and over the cattle,
> and over all the earth, and over every creeping thing that
> creepeth upon the earth. So God created man in his *own*
> image, in the image of God created he him; male and
> female created he them."

Notice God speaks of Himself in the plural—"our"—and then back to the singular—"his" and "he." The next reference to the trinity is in Genesis 3:22:

> "And the LORD God said, Behold, the man is become as one of us, to know good and evil…"

Again, God refers to Himself in the singular and the plural. Also, consider the following:

ALL CALLED GOD

FATHER:	John 6:27
SON:	Psalms 45:6,7
	John 20:28
	1Timothy 1:16,17
HOLY SPIRIT:	Acts 5:3,4

ALL HAVE DIVINE ATTRIBUTES

FATHER:	James 1:17
SON:	Hebrews 13:8
HOLY SPIRIT	John 6:63
	Hebrews 9:14

ALL PERFORM DIVINE WORKS

FATHER:	John 5:21
SON:	John 5:21
HOLY SPIRIT:	Romans 8:11

EACH RECEIVES DIVINE HONORS

FATHER:	John 5:23
	2Corinthians 13:14

SON: John 5:23
                            2Corinthians 13:14
HOLY SPIRIT: 2Corinthians 13:14

Christ is one member of the Holy Trinity—God the Father, God the Son and God the Holy Spirit. The first reference to the Holy Trinity in the New Testament is found in Matthew 3:16,17: "And Jesus, when He was baptized, went up straightway out of the water and lo the heavens were opened unto Him and He saw the Spirit of God descending like a dove and lighting upon Him, and lo a voice from heaven saying, This is my beloved Son in whom I am well pleased." Another is found in 2 Corinthians 13:14: "The grace of the Lord Jesus Christ and the love of God and the communion of the Holy Ghost be with you all, Amen." Also: "But we are bound to give thanks alway to God for you brethren, beloved of the Lord, because God hath from the beginning chosen you to salvation through sanctification of the Spirit and belief of the truth" (2 Thes. 2:13). In 1 Peter 1:2, we are told; "Elect according to the foreknowledge of God the Father, through sanctification of the Spirit, unto obedience and sprinkling of the blood of Jesus Christ..." In Matthew 28:19, Jesus said:

> "Go ye therefore and teach all nations baptizing them
> in the name of the Father and of the Son and of the Holy
> Ghost."

I believe God is one in three persons. Each person of the Godhead is an individual person and yet all three are God. I don't know how this is possible. I believe there are some things the human mind cannot understand, as I demonstrated earlier. This is one of them. Another is how God could create the universe out of nothing. He said He did but He did not explain how, other than to say by the word of His mouth (Ps 33:6,9), which doesn't fill in the details enough for me to understand exactly how it was done. Therefore I am left with accepting what God has chosen to reveal.

Tohu and bohu

Genesis 1:2 tells us: "And the earth was without form and void and darkness was upon the face of the deep. And the Spirit of God moved upon the face of the waters." The words "without form and void" are translated from the Hebrew words tohu and bohu. Some believe this describes the first stage in creation where there is the inevitable chaos and confusion visible at any construction site. When man creates something there is always the tohu and bohu in the beginning. But when God creates there is none of that. In Psalm 33:6,9 we are told: "By the word of the LORD were the heavens made and all the host of them by the breath of His mouth...For He spake and it was done, He commanded and it stood fast." The only other place where the two words, tohu and bohu appear together is in Jeremiah 4:23: "I beheld the earth and lo it was without form and void, and the heavens, and they had no light." The formless and empty condition exists here as the result of the sins of the Israelites. In Job 38:6,7 God tells Job that the morning stars sang together and all the sons of God shouted for joy at the creation. Tohu and bohu also mean an indistinguishable ruin and confusion, and yet in 1 Corinthians 14:33 we learn that God is not the author of confusion.

Another explanation of Genesis 1:2 is that the scene of indistinguishable ruin and confusion described there is the result of sin as is also described in Jeremiah 4:23. But who sinned? Who caused the condition found in verse two? Those who believe this believe that an unrevealed period of time elapsed between verse one and two. This is often referred to as the Gap Theory. During this time Satan and his angels caused the condition found in verse two after they rebelled and were cast out of heaven down to the earth. This view makes more sense to me after considering the above scriptures. Also, if there was no time gap between Genesis 1:1 and 1:2, then when did Satan have time to rebel?

Critics of the Gap Theory believe sin originated in the Garden of Eden, not before, and their favorite verse to support their belief is in Romans 5:12: "Wherefore, as by one man sin entered into the world, and death by sin; and so death passed upon all men, for that all have sinned" (see also 1 Cor. 15:21). This verse does not say sin and death *originated* in the Garden of Eden, rather this is where they first made their appearance in what Peter calls "the world that then was" as opposed to the present age: "For this they willingly are ignorant of, that by the word of God the heavens were of old, and the earth standing out of the water and in the water: Whereby the world that then was, being overflowed with water, perished" (2 Pet. 3:5, 6).

If sin originated in the Garden of Eden, where did Satan and his angels have time to rebel, be judged and be cast down to the earth? Surely all that didn't occur in the six days of creation, did it? Satan is portrayed as well established in the Garden. The Gap Theory provides an unrevealed length of time for such a significant historical tragedy.

CHAPTER TWO

PROVING GOD EXISTS

When we set out to explain why and how something happens, we must use the evidence, facts and experience available to us if we are to arrive at a logical conclusion. Using available evidence, experience, facts, observation and experimentation, we know that the universe had a beginning and that before that beginning there was no universe and therefore there was nothing. We know this because of the Law of Causality (for every effect there is a cause). Based on this law, we can use the following logic:

> 1. The universe exists.
> 2. The universe had a beginning.
> 3. Before the beginning of the universe, there was no universe.
> 4. Since there was no universe, there was nothing.
> 5. Something never comes from nothing by any natural cause.
> 6. Since the universe does exist, it came from nothing.
> 7. Therefore the cause of the universe is supernatural.
> 8. Life exists.
> 9. Life always comes from pre-existing life of the same kind (the Law of Biogenesis).
> 10. Life cannot come from nonliving matter by any natural cause.
> 11. Since life does exist, the cause of life is supernatural.

Many people with a naturalistic worldview assume everything can be explained by natural causes. From the beginning they reject the possibility of a supernatural cause. Because of this they are left with no scientifically valid answers to the question of how the universe could come from nothing, which is impossible by any natural cause of which we are aware. Many answers have been proposed that go beyond the realm of known evidence, experience, facts, observation and experimentation and therefore enter the realm of fiction.

The same logic applies to life. Using available evidence, experience, facts, observation and experimentation we know that life only comes from pre-existing life of the same kind.

> *"Spontaneous generation (the emergence of life from nonliving matter) has never been observed. All observations have shown that life comes only from life. This has been observed so consistently it is called the Law of Biogenesis. Evolution conflicts with this scientific law by claiming that life came from nonliving matter through natural processes"*
> (From *In the Beginning* by Walt Brown, Ph.D. page 5).

Life never comes from non-living matter by any natural cause of which we are aware.

Is God the Author of the Bible?

Now that we have seen proof that God exists, using logic based on known evidence, experience, facts, observation and experimentation, we need to see if He has revealed Himself to us. In the Holy Bible there are hundreds of prophecies given by God who is speaking in the first person. In both Bible and secular history we find that those prophecies have been accurately fulfilled. No other writing on earth comes close to doing this! Only God can accurately reveal the future, therefore He is the author of the Holy Bible. Within the pages of the Holy Bible He reveals His nature, our nature, His relationship to us, our need for salvation and His plan of salvation for us.

The reason the universe and life cannot come from nothing by any natural cause but can come from a supernatural cause is because God is the self-existent creator of everything and everyone. He is not subject to His creation. He created it and sustains it. It is a mistake to judge God by human standards and human perspectives. God reveals that He is omnipotent, omniscient and omnipresent.

If you are interested in more detailed proof read, *Evidence that Demands a Verdict* by Josh McDowell.

Objections

I have shared the above information with a number of people and have received some interesting responses:

[1]

"You're an idiot."

He may have a point there but his critique of my idiotic conclusions seems to be rather brief.

[2]

These conclusions seem to be logical. The only idea that sticks out to me as being odd is, "Since there was no universe, there was nothing." I'm trying to figure out how one might conclude that if there is no universe, there must be nothing at all. However, I don't suppose that if there were something outside of or apart from the universe (that was also the cause of the universe) we would be able to understand it or come to any concrete conclusions regarding it's nature, as it would likely not be subject to the physical and natural laws contained within the universe (unless it was contained within a universe with the same physical laws, but that would give rise to the original question once again). All things considered, whatever did cause the universe must be super-natural, since super-natural means beyond nature or outside of nature (nature being the universe), so I suppose I have no option but to agree. However, I think that your 4th logical point should be re-worded to say something like "Since there was no universe, there was nothing submissive to the laws of nature."

"Many people with a naturalistic worldview assume everything can be explained by natural causes. From the beginning, they reject the possibility of a supernatural cause. Because of this they are left with no scientifically valid answers to the question of how the universe could come from nothing, which is impossible by any natural cause of which we are aware. Many answers have been proposed that go beyond the realm of known evidence, facts and experience and therefore enter the realm of fiction."

Again, everything seems logical to me. The only thing that bothers me about this paragraph is your usage of the word "fiction". If you are correct that "fiction" is the right word to use here, then all other beliefs (including your own) must also be described as "fiction" since they go "beyond the realm of known evidence, facts and experience . . ." I think perhaps you should use the word "belief" instead of "fiction".

"Now that we have seen proof that God exists, using logic based on known facts, we need to see if He has revealed Himself to us. In the Holy Bible there are hundreds of prophecies given by God who is speaking in the first person. In both Bible and secular history we find that those prophecies have been fulfilled. No other writing on earth comes close to doing this! Only God can accurately reveal the future, therefore, He is the author of the Holy Bible. Within the pages of the Holy Bible He reveals His nature, our nature, His relationship to us and His plan of salvation for us.

"The reason the universe and life cannot come from nothing by any natural cause, but can come from a supernatural cause is because God is the self-existent creator of everything and everyone. He is not subject to His creation. He created it and sustains it. It is a mistake to judge God by human standards and human perspectives. God reveals that He is omnipotent, omniscient and omnipresent."

As I said, I do agree that there must be something other than nature (super-natural) in order for the universe to exist, but what that something's attributes are must logically remain a matter of speculation (since they are unprovable). I believe theism (and many theistic beliefs) to be extremely reasonable. Your own belief seems very reasonable to me, but what you have given us is not conclusive evidence, it is some of the reasons you believe what you believe. Perhaps what you were looking for was someone to agree that your belief is reasonable, well you've got it. More power to ya.

I appreciate an occasional encouragement no matter how rare but I wonder about some of the statements made by this person. His statement that "I'm trying to figure out how one might conclude that 'if there is no universe, there must be nothing at all,'" is a little hard for me to understand, since the definition of 'universe' is everything that exists. In our experience, if nothing exists, there is nothing. Also, I believe we can safely assume that before the existence of everything, there was nothing. I fail to understand why that is such a hard concept to grasp and yet it is one of the most common objections I received.

The next thing he objected to is my use of the word "fiction" rather than "belief." As I point out, when we depart from the principles of basic science—evidence, experience, facts, observation and experimentation—we enter the realm of fiction. Also, his statement that what I have presented goes beyond the realm of known evidence, facts and experience, seems incorrect. If our understanding of reality is based on our concept of known evidence, facts and experience, then it seems to me our understanding should be pretty close to reality. It seems to me that fiction departs from that understanding. Science fiction is fun to read but even though a story may use some scientific principles, it does go off into unrealistic speculation.

My respondent says he finds everything to be logical, but at the same time he has trouble accepting some of the logic. He claims that knowing the attributes of the supernatural cause of the universe and life is "unprovable." I thought I did a fair job of proving God's attributes by proving He authored the Holy

Bible because of the existence of hundreds of accurately fulfilled prophecies. After that we can confidently believe the accuracy of what He chooses to reveal to us about Himself in His written word.

Except for those few objections this response was very positive and welcome. I wish I could say the same for the vast majority. However they were stimulating and caused me to re-examine my conclusions, so they were also welcome. Here are a few more:

[3]

"We know this because of the Law of Causality (for every cause there is an effect and for every effect there is a cause)."

It is, at least, highly debatable as to whether there exists any real causality at the quantum level.

"1. The universe exists."
"2. The universe had a beginning."

Agreed.

"3. Before the beginning of the universe, there was no universe."

Logical contradiction. Time is a property of the universe. Hence, any usage of the word "before" must, by definition, be in reference to something that is within the universe. There is no "before" the universe—it doesn't make sense.

"4. Since there was no universe, there was nothing."

That contradicts your conclusion (point 7). If there was nothing, then there cannot have been a cause, whether natural or supernatural, can there?

"5. Something never comes from nothing by any natural cause."

Of course, if there was nothing then there cannot have been a cause, natural or otherwise. However, nothing *can* come from nothing without a cause, as demonstrated by quantum vacuum fluctuations.

"6. Since the universe does exist, it came from nothing."

Re-statement of points 1 through 4.

"7. The cause of the universe is supernatural."

This contradicts point 4.

"8. Life exists."

Agreed.

"9. Life always comes from pre-existing life of the same kind (the Law of Biogenesis)."

No such law exists. We have no precise definition of what life actually is, let alone what "kinds" of life are. Besides, this would contradict your conclusion.

"10. Life cannot come from nonliving matter by any natural cause."

Why not?

"11. Since life does exist, the cause of life is supernatural."

Contradicts point 9.

This person begins his objections by appealing to quantum mechanics as if it were a firmly established scientific fact rather than the questionable and debatable concept it really is. R.C. Sproul has some interesting comments about quantum mechanics in his book *Not a Chance*. He is not a scientist, but he is a logician and he points out how illogical it is to assume that because an electron seems to vanish at one level and reappear at another, therefore matter appears from nothing.

Another good resource is "Who Created God" by Jonathan Sarfati. Here is an excerpt:

"Quantum mechanics never produces something out of nothing. Theories that the universe is a quantum fluctuation must presuppose that there was something to fluctuate—their 'quantum vacuum' is a lot of matter-antimatter potential—not 'nothing'."

My respondent's comments about time are interesting, but flawed. Let me share an explanation from a source that says it much better than I can:

"If God is eternal, when did He create the world? This asks a confused question. Being in time, we can imagine a moment before the beginning of time, yet there really was no such moment. God did not create the world in time; He is responsible for the creation of time. There was no time 'before' time. There was only eternity. The word 'when' assumes that there was a time before time. This is like asking, 'Where was the man when he jumped off the bridge?' On the bridge? That was before he jumped. In the air? That was after. In this question, 'when' assumes a definite point for a process action. Jumping is the process of going from the bridge to the air. In the question about Creation, it tries to put God into time rather than starting it. We can speak of a creation of time, but not in time." (*When Skeptics Ask* by Norman L, Geisler and Ronald M. Brooks, pp 31, 32).

The rest of my respondent's objections seem to be based more on denial than science. I suppose it is encouraging that he at least agrees that the universe exists, had a beginning and that life exists. I suppose that is a starting point of sorts. He asks "why not?" to my statement that life cannot come from non-living matter by any natural cause. He must have read my explanation with his eyes closed—or his mind, more likely. Here is another one:

[4]

> **"3. Before the beginning of the universe, there was no universe."**
> **"4. Since there was no universe, there was nothing."**

These points you might have to take up with Stephen Hawking, as he is currently working on theories describing the state of reality prior to the Big Bang. The currently accepted theory of a singularity igniting the universe is well founded with vast amounts of supporting evidence, so one might claim that a pre-universe would be a Singularity. Regardless, these two points are without evidence supporting them.

> **"5. Something never comes from nothing by any natural cause."**

Wrong. Do a little search through some cosmology journals (there are many, and several are probably available in your local library) for "Zero-Point Energy."

Now, my argument isn't in support of Zero-Point energy (it is still far too controversial for me to begin to argue), but my argument is for the process by which Zero-Point energy is hypothesized to be possible and also the means by which black holes "evaporate."

In the Universe, there is fluctuation. This fluctuation is caused by an interesting universal phenomenon: subatomic particles spontaneously spawn and annihilate with their antiparticles in otherwise "empty" space. For reference, see: Stephen Hawking's "A Brief History of Time" for a solid explanation of the phenomenon.

This little factoid, in disarming the truth-value of 5, renders conclusions 6 and 7 false, giving you an unsound argument through to point 7.

"9. Life always comes from pre-existing life of the same kind (the Law of Biogenesis)."

"10. Life cannot come from nonliving matter by any natural cause."

False. See: Dawkins, Richard "The Blind Watchmaker." He explains the competing camps of abiogenesis and how biogenesis is possible—and indeed probable—from nonliving matter. We see self-replication in salt crystallization with modification for changing circumstances. We see crystalline structures ideal for "cookie cutters" for life. We see the perfect habitat for the foundation of life in the foam of the sea and the bottom of the ocean in dark, volcanic vents. It is entirely possible.

This makes the conclusion of point 11 unsound and invalid.

Using Ockham's Razor as a guide, your argument falls short of the necessary validity and truth to convince anyone even mildly skeptical that there is, in fact, a god.

This respondent places most of his objections on the speculation and hypotheses of Zero-Point Energy (which he admits is still far too controversial for him to begin to argue) and "*The Blind Watchmaker*," which he describes as "possible—and indeed probable."

His claim that the action of salt crystallization and crystalline structures somehow produces some ideal situation for the production of life from non-living matter seems like quite a stretch to me. Is he claiming to know what is the ideal situation for the production of life from non-living matter? Does anyone have this information? Also, what in the world is he talking about when he claims that sea foam and the dark, volcanic vents on the sea bottom somehow create the "perfect habitat for the foundation of life?" First of all, is he saying he, or anyone, knows what perfect habitat for the emergence of life is required to produce life from non-living matter? These notions are easy to say, but have never been demonstrated so far, and probably never will be. This is the sort of thing I mean by resorting to fiction to try to defend a scientifically unsound belief.

He ends by revealing that he uses Ockham's Razor as his guide to conclude that my entire argument falls apart. What is Ockham's Razor? It is the principle proposed by William of Ockham in the fourteenth century that "entities should not be multiplied unnecessarily," or keep it simple. I don't see how that philosophy makes my entire argument fall apart. Here again it seems we are confronted with denial of self-evident facts from which we can draw logical conclusions.

I have chosen to answer my next respondent's objections point-by-point:

[5]

"1. The universe exists" (On this we agree).

It is encouraging to see we agree on this point.

"2. The universe had a beginning" (This has yet to be proven and, philosophically, is unlikely).

Dr. Walt Brown does a good job of answering that objection:

> "The first law of thermodynamics states that the total energy in the universe, or in any isolated part of it, remains constant. In other words, energy (or its mass equivalent) is not now being created or destroyed; it is simply changing form. Countless experiments have verified this. A corollary of the first law is that natural processes cannot create energy. Consequently, energy must have been created in the past by some agency or power outside and independent of the natural universe. Furthermore, if natural processes cannot produce mass and energy—the relatively simple inorganic portion of the universe—then it is even less likely that natural processes can explain the much more complex organic (or living) portion of the universe.
>
> "If the entire universe is an isolated system, then, according to the second law of thermodynamics, the

energy in the universe available for useful work has always been decreasing. However, as one goes back in time, the energy available for useful work would eventually exceed the total energy in the universe that, according to the first law of thermodynamics, remains constant. This is an impossible condition, thus implying the universe had a beginning" (*In the Beginning* by Walt Brown, Ph.D. pp 24, 25).

"3. Before the beginning of the universe, there was no universe" (True, if there was an actual beginning. Otherwise, this is false).

Glad to see we agree on this point.

"4. Since there was no universe, there was nothing" (If there was ever nothing, than there was also no "God", as every existent is a something).

That assertion has been rationally answered many times. Here is an excellent precise and to-the-point example in my opinion:

"This question comes up a lot. The problem is that people don't listen well to what we have to say. We didn't say that everything needs a cause; we said everything that has a beginning needs a cause. Only finite, contingent things need a cause. God didn't have a beginning; He is infinite and He is necessary. God is the uncaused cause of all finite things. If God needed a cause, we would begin an infinite regress of causes that would never answer the question. As it is, we can't ask, "Who caused God?" because God is the first cause. You can't go back any farther than a first" (*When Skeptics Ask* by Norman L. Geisler and Ronald M. Brooks p 29).

"5. Something never comes from nothing by any natural cause" (True, but there is no other kind of cause—except as I have explained (and even that occurs within the confines of the natural)).

His assertion that there is no other cause than natural is based on a preconception that is evidence free, illogical and false. Since he agrees that the universe does exist, and since I have proven it had to have a beginning, and since I have proven that before that beginning there was nothing, and since he agrees that something never comes from nothing by any natural cause, then we are left with a supernatural cause for the universe, which he is actually agreeing with, even though he doesn't seem to realize it.

"6. Since the universe does exist, it came from nothing" (This is a contradiction of your 5th point).

Where is the contradiction? My statement in point 5 includes "by any natural cause." Apparently that fact, which is assumed in point 6, escaped him.

"7. The cause of the universe is supernatural" (There is nothing (ultimately) outside of nature and nothing above or beyond it—no room at all for the supernatural. The word is self-contradicting).

Then explain to me what natural cause produced everything that exists—from nothing. He reveals by his assertion that it is probably based on nothing more than his pre-conception that God does not exist, since he offers no supporting evidence.

"8. Life exists" (Obviously).

Eureka! Another agreement!

"9. Life always comes from pre-existing life of the same kind (the Law of Biogenesis)" (Not proven).

But it has been proved numerous times. Here is another example:

"There was a time when people thought that life could generate itself 'spontaneously' from the earth. For example, people believed that worms just 'popped' out of the mud. But through careful observations, scientists refuted that idea. It was demonstrated through experimentation as far back as 1668 by Italian physician Francesco Redi. Redi showed that maggots do not generate spontaneously on meat, but instead come from flies.

"Later, in 1860, one year after Darwin published his book on evolution, The Origin of Species, French chemist Louis Pasteur did a series of experiments. Pasteur proved that microorganisms appear from air-born sources and not 'spontaneously.' This laid to rest the controversy over spontaneous generation. The Law of Biogenesis was confirmed.

"The Law of Biogenesis states that life only comes from pre-existing life. In other words, 'You don't get something living from something dead.' This is one of the most fundamental laws of biology. It has never been refuted. All of our experience confirms this law to be true. Worms come from other worms, not from 'dead' mud. Babies come from living parents. Mold on bread comes from pre-existing mold spores in the air.

"Since the law of biogenesis is confirmed, then why do evolutionists insist that life originated from non-living matter? Isn't that a contradiction? YES, it is! It contradicts everything we know to be true about living plants and animals! Then why do some scientists continue to believe in evolution when its very foundation goes against this well-known law of science?" (*Science and the Origin of Life* by Chuck Edwards from Summit Ministries).

"10. Life cannot come from nonliving matter by any natural cause" (Again, not proven).

Wrong! See point 9.

"11. Since life does exist, the cause of life is supernatural"
(Necessarily false, see above reasons. Also, isn't your
"God" supposed to be living? If so, your "logic" would
necessarily apply to It as well).

Again, he errs. See my explanation at point 9. First he refers to
his "above reasons," which are nothing but evidence free denials.
Then he attempts to change the subject. It is revealing that he refers
to God as It, but it is encouraging that at least he does condescend
to capitalize the I. Concerning the beginning of God:

> *"Again, only finite, contingent beings need causes.*
> *Necessary beings don't. We never said that God is a*
> *self-caused Being. That would be impossible. However,*
> *we can turn this objection into an argument for God.*
> *There are only three possible kinds of being: self-caused,*
> *caused by another, and uncaused. Which are we?*
> *Self-caused is impossible with respect to existence;*
> *we can't bring ourselves into existence* [nor can God!].
> *Uncaused would mean that we are necessary, eternal,*
> *infinite beings, which we are not; so we must be caused*
> *by another. If we are caused by another, what kind of*
> *being is He? Again, self-caused is impossible; if He were*
> *caused by another, that leads to an infinite regress; so*
> *He must be uncaused"* (*When Skeptics Ask* by Norman
> L. Geisler and Ronald M. Brooks p 29).

My conclusion from these and many other objections that are
pretty much along the same lines is that those who are determined
to believe God does not exist will continue to believe what they
want to believe despite facts and logic. They begin with the
dogmatic presumption that God does not exist and no amount of
factual information will move them from that position.

With NO scientific evidence, why do so many "scientists" embrace evolution? Following are some quotes from noted evolutionists, which will shed light on this subject:

H.G. Wells, author and historian, wrote: *"If all animals and man evolved . . . then the entire historic fabric of Christianity—the story of the first sin and the reason for an atonement—collapsed like a house of cards."* (*The Outline of History*)

Aldous Huxley stated the matter succinctly in his article, "Confessions of a Professed Atheist": *"I had motives for not wanting the world to have meaning; consequently, assumed it had none, and was able without any difficulty to find reasons for this assumption . . . The philosopher who finds no meaning in the world is not concerned exclusively with a problem in pure metaphysics; he is also concerned to prove there is no valid reason why he personally should not do as he wants to do . . . For myself, as no doubt for most of my contemporaries, the philosophy of meaninglessness was essentially an instrument of liberation. The liberation we desired was simultaneously liberation from a certain political and economic system and liberation from a certain system of morality. We objected to the morality because it interfered with our sexual freedom"* (1966, 3:19).

The late Sir Julian Huxley, once the world's leading evolution "expert", and head of the United Nations Educational Scientific Cultural Organization (UNESCO), In answer to the question on the Merv Griffin show: 'Why do people believe in evolution?' said, *"The reason we accepted Darwinism even without proof, is because we didn't want God to interfere with our sexual mores."*

George Wald, another prominent Evolutionist (a Harvard University biochemist and Nobel Laureate), wrote, *"When it comes to the Origin of Life there are only two possibilities: creation or spontaneous generation. There is no third way. Spontaneous generation was disproved one hundred years ago, but that leads us to only one other conclusion, that of supernatural creation. We cannot accept that on philosophical grounds; therefore, we choose to believe the impossible: that life arose spontaneously by chance!"* ("The Origin of Life," *Scientific American,* 191:48, May 1954).

According to *their own testimonies,* some of the most prominent evolutionists believed and taught evolution, NOT because of any scientific evidence, but *based upon their rejection of God.*

CHAPTER THREE

SATAN

Who is Satan and where did he come from? The first reference to Satan is found in Genesis 3 in the story of Adam and Eve being persuaded by the serpent to eat the forbidden fruit. In Revelation 12:9 we are told that the serpent was Satan. There are some problems with the story of Satan that lead me to believe he is not a literal person, but rather the symbolic personification of unredeemed, rebellious human nature.

Cursed by God

In Genesis 3:14, in the Garden of Eden, Satan the serpent is cursed by God to crawl on his belly and eat dust all the days of his life. One explanation I have heard from those who insist on taking this story literally is the serpent was not talking at all. After all, they say, it does not have vocal cords. So they explain it by claiming Satan was hiding in the bushes behind the serpent and using ventriloquism to make Eve think it was talking. There are at least three reasons this does not make sense:

> ➤ 1. Revelation 12:9 says the serpent *was* Satan.
> ➤ 2. The story says nothing about a ventriloquist Satan.
> ➤ 3. If that explanation is true then God was also deceived since he cursed the serpent, not Satan.

We next hear about Satan rising up and inciting David to take a census of Israel in 1 Chronicles 21:1. Not a bad trick for someone whom God has cursed to crawl on his belly in the form of a snake, but that account is mild compared to the story in Job. Here we find Satan mingling with the angels of heaven, talking to God, and actually making a bet with God that he can make Job curse God to His face if he is allowed to hurt him and kill his children, servants and livestock. In the story God becomes an accessory with Satan—a partner—in an unspeakable crime against a man whom God has described as His servant who is blameless, upright, fears God and shuns evil (Job 1:6-12).

Is Job literal?

In 2 Corinthians 6:14,15, we are told:

> "Be ye not unequally yoked together with unbelievers, for what fellowship hath righteousness with unrighteousness and what communion hath light with darkness and what communion hath Christ with Belial?"

If the story of Job really happened, then it seems we have a conflict in Scripture with the nature of God. On the one hand we are told that Christ (God) can have no harmony with Belial, but the story of Job tells us just the opposite. Because of this conflict, I believe the book of Job is a parable or allegory about the age-old problem of good people suffering misfortune and tragedy. The conversations recorded in this book are attempts to explain this problem from a human perspective. Finally God speaks to Job and his friends telling them they don't know what they are talking about (Job 38:1,2). Job's family is never mentioned in any genealogy or anywhere else in Scripture. In Ezekiel 14:14,20 God mentions Job: "Though these three men, Noah, Daniel and Job, were in it, they should deliver but their own souls by their righteousness...though Noah, Daniel, and Job were in it . . . they shall deliver neither son nor daughter; they shall but deliver their own souls by their righteousness." Job is mentioned one other time in James 5:11: "Ye have heard of the patience of Job..." The fact that Job is mentioned thee times outside of the book of Job does not necessarily mean the story is literal. He could appear in a parable and still be referred to as an example of virtue. I might compare a weight lifter's build with Superman's physique, or I might say someone is as strong as Atlas. On the other hand Job could have been a real person in history who experienced the tragedies described, and the parable was based on his life to deal with the age-old question of why good people suffer.

The beginning of Satan

Many believe the beginning of Satan is described in Isaiah 14 and Ezekiel 28. In Isaiah, God is prophesying against the king of Babylon whom He describes in symbolic language at times, especially in verses 12-14. In verse 12 the name Lucifer is used, giving rise to the belief that Satan's original name was Lucifer and was changed to Satan after he fell. Lucifer is a Latin word translated from the Hebrew expression "morning star" and left un-translated from Latin into English in the King James and some other translations. Incidentally, Jesus is described as the bright and morning star in Revelation 22:16. In Isaiah 15 through 20 God goes on to describe this man's fate. Note that in verse 16 those who gazed on his body referred to him as a man: "Is this the man that made the earth to tremble..." This is hardly the picture of a heavenly immortal being who is supposed to still be doing evil today. This king has been dead for over two thousand years.

In Ezekiel 28 God is describing another king whom He raised up and then destroyed because of his sins. Verse 12 clearly states this is a lament concerning the king of Tyre and yet many believe He is speaking about Satan. Verses 12 through 17 use symbolic language that even seems to place the king in Eden. Dropping down to verses 18 and 19 we read: "Thou hast defiled thy sanctuaries by the multitude of thine iniquities, by the iniquity of thy traffic, therefore will I bring forth a fire from the midst of thee, it shall devour thee and I will bring thee to ashes upon the earth in the sight of all them that behold thee. All they that know thee among the people shall be astonished at thee. Thou shalt be a terror, and never shalt thou be any more." This king of Tyre also died over two thousand years ago.

Let us also consider something else in this chapter. If it is really talking about the beginning of Satan, then he must have originated before the Garden of Eden. But in verses 18 and 19 God destroyed him. That means he never made it to the Garden in order to tempt Eve. Also when did Satan and his rebel angels have time to rebel and be thrown down to earth if the timeline is continuous and uninterrupted from Genesis 1:1? By the time he is introduced in the Garden of Eden, he is well established.

According to Revelation 20:10, ". . . the devil that deceived them was cast into the lake of fire and brimstone, where the beast and the false prophet are, and shall be tormented day and night for ever and ever." Is Satan going to be tormented forever in the lake of fire in the sense that he and all the wicked will be tormented throughout all eternity without end? Revelation does seem to be saying that, but if it means what it seems to mean, then it seems to be contradicting those passages above in Isaiah and Ezekiel, if they really are speaking of Satan, since they tell us he is to come to an end. Other scriptures tell us sin is to be forever removed from God's creation.

Sin will be eradicated

Consider the following:

> ➤ "He [God] will make an utter end. Affliction shall not rise up the second time" (Nahum 1:9).

> ➤ "For behold, I create new heavens and a new earth, and the former shall not be remembered nor come into mind" (Isa. 65:17).

> ➤ "And God shall wipe away all tears from their eyes, and there shall be no more death, neither sorrow nor crying, neither shall there be any more pain" (Rev. 21:4).

If there is to remain a lake of fire where the wicked are to reside forever screaming in torment, then it seems to me that sin has not been removed but only isolated, which would contradict these and other verses.

I am inclined to believe that the lake of fire mentioned in Revelation 19:20 and 20:10, is not the same kind of fire on which we cook. Jesus tells us to:

> ". . . fear not them which kill the body, but are not
> able to kill the soul, but rather fear Him which is able to
> destroy both soul and body in hell" (Mt. 10:28).

Men have killed many people with fire, but according to Jesus, that fire was not able to kill their souls. The lake of fire kills both body and soul; therefore the lake of fire must be symbolic of some spiritual fire capable of destroying souls. Or perhaps the lake of fire is simply symbolic of the total cleansing of sin from God's creation. In Matthew 25:41,46 Jesus said:

> "Then shall he say also unto them on the left hand,
> Depart from me, ye cursed, into **everlasting fire**,
> prepared for the devil and his angels…And these shall
> go away into everlasting punishment: but the righteous
> into life eternal."

Some think Jesus is confirming everlasting torment but not really. He says nothing here about torment and He mentions everlasting *punishment* not everlasting *punishing.* The punishment of eternal death (which is the opposite of "life eternal") is everlasting.

The word "forever" as used in the Bible simply means a period of time, limited or unlimited. It is used 56 times in the Bible in connection with things that have already ended. It is like the word "large" which means something different in describing men, trees, or mountains. In Jonah 2:6, "forever" means "three days and nights." In Deuteronomy 23:3 it means "ten generations." In the case of man, it means "as he lives" or "until death" (See

Ex. 21:6; 1 Sam. 1:22,28). So the wicked will burn in the fire as long as they live, or until they perish (John 3:16). I would not be surprised to learn that the teaching of eternal torment has done more to drive people to false religions, atheism and insanity than any other invention of men. It is slander upon the loving character of a caring, tender, gracious heavenly Father and has probably done untold harm to the understanding and acceptance of truth.

Did God commit murder?

I occasionally hear someone accuse God of committing murder. This charge is usually based on the account of the worldwide flood, the command to totally wipe out every man woman and child in Jericho, the Promised Land, etc. At first glance, it does seem that this charge has merit. We regularly condemn anyone or nation that commits this kind of atrocity, and there is ample evidence in history where this has happened. Nazi Germany comes to mind with the murder of six million Jews. Mao of China and the leaders of the Soviet Union murdered over 100,000,000 innocent people. Muslim terrorists are currently on a worldwide rampage of murder.

But what about God? Does He fall into the same category? Can we judge Him by the same standards that we judge one another? First, let's define murder. Murder is the deliberate, premeditated killing of an innocent human being by another human being. I think we can also say that if God deliberately took the life of an innocent human being that would also be murder. Admittedly, there are a few times recorded in the Holy Bible where God takes the life of babies or commands others to do so. I think the key word in the definition of murder is "innocent." From our limited perspective, babies are the most innocent people on earth. If it is true that each baby is a new creation, I believe we would be correct. But suppose reincarnation is true and all of humanity was created at the same time thousands or millions of years ago? If that is true, then it is also true that every baby has lived many times in the past and is born with a load of past sins. Therefore, there is no such thing as an innocent baby, or anyone else, from God's perspective.

Also, God defines murder as sin and commands the death penalty for the murderer. If God commits murder He is guilty of sin, isn't He? Does anyone really believe God is capable of sin? No, God is not a sinner. He is totally righteous and does not tolerate sin. He judges sin and when He destroyed wicked people and nations He was exercising righteous judgment against the wicked. Personally I am thankful God is righteous and judges the wicked. If you think about it, so are most people. Don't we all cheer the destruction of the wicked? I was thankful for the destruction of Nazism and the Soviet Union. And I continue to cheer every time another Muslim terrorist is killed or captured.

A strange act

God's judgment on the wicked is described in Isaiah 28:21 as a strange act: "For the LORD shall rise up . . . that He may do His work, His strange work, and bring to pass His act, His strange act." In Ezekiel 33:11 God says: "As I live, saith the Lord GOD, I have no pleasure in the death of the wicked, but that the wicked turn from his way and live." If God has no pleasure in the death of the wicked, is it reasonable that He would torture them forever? Scripture says that the wicked:

➤ Shall suffer destruction	(Job 21:3)
➤ Shall be burned up	(Mal. 4:1)
➤ Shall be devoured	(Ps. 21:9)
➤ Shall be cut off	(Ps. 37:9)
➤ Shall be consumed	(Ps. 37:20)
➤ Shall be destroyed together	(Ps. 37:38)
➤ Shall be slain	(Ps. 62:3)
➤ Shall be destroyed	(Ps. 145:20)
➤ Shall suffer death	(Rom. 6:23)

Satan's origin

People seem to be determined to make those verses in Isaiah and Ezekiel describe Satan's origin. But in order to do so, they have to change the accounts from literally speaking of known kings, to symbolically speaking about Satan, then back again. I don't recall any other place in Scripture where this sort of flip-flop takes place.

If these passages in Isaiah and Ezekiel don't tell us where Satan came from, where else can we turn? The only place I have found anything about Satan's alleged origin is in Revelation 12:3,4,7-9:

> "And there appeared another wonder in heaven and behold; a great red dragon having seven heads and ten horns, and seven crowns upon his heads. And his tail drew the third part of the stars of heaven and did cast them to the earth. And the dragon stood before the woman which was ready to be delivered, for to devour her child as soon as it was born . . . And there was war in heaven; Michael and his angels fought against the dragon and the dragon fought and his angels and prevailed not, neither was their place found any more in heaven. And the great dragon was cast out, that old serpent called the Devil, and Satan, which deceiveth the whole world. He was cast out into the earth and his angels were cast out with him."

That is not exactly an origin, but it is the closest I can think of. This passage is highly symbolical. Remember that Satan, "that old serpent" was supposed to be under a curse from God to crawl on his belly eating dust for the rest of his days. When was that curse lifted, so that he could appear again in heaven to war against Michael and the angels? Surely Satan couldn't ignore a curse from God, could he?

The reference to Satan drawing a third of the stars out of heaven and casting them to the earth is evidently the only reference justifying the doctrine of a third of the angels following Satan in his rebellion against God. The stars here are seen as representing angels. This idea can be justified from Revelation 1:20: "The mystery of the seven stars which thou sawest in My right hand, and the seven golden candlesticks. The seven stars are the angels of the seven churches . . ."

These verses seem pretty flimsy to me for building a doctrine of the origin of Satan. However, they do seem to be the strongest evidence that Scripture has to offer. Satan and/or the devil are mentioned 19 times in the Old Testament and 94 times in the New Testament. Many of these references are to "a devil" or "devils" rather than Satan himself. Christ mentioned Satan several times. After Christ's 72 disciples returned from their missionary journey rejoicing at all the wonderful miracles they had performed in His name He said, "I beheld Satan as lightning fall from heaven" (Lk. 10:18). I believe this was a euphemistic way of joyfully exclaiming, "Wow! Right on! Great! Good work!" rather than a literal statement of Satan's fall since that wouldn't fit the context. Why would Jesus pick that moment to talk about an event that must have occurred before Genesis 1:2? Even though I do not believe in a literal person named Satan, I do believe in literal demons which I believe are disincarnate entities. I'll go into greater detail about that later.

Is Peter Satan?

Another statement about Satan is found in Matthew. Jesus had been revealing to His disciples that He was going to have to suffer and be killed by the authorities. "Then Peter took Him and began to rebuke Him saying, Be it far from Thee Lord, this shall not be unto Thee. But He turned and said unto Peter:

> "Get thee behind Me Satan! Thou art an offence unto
> Me. For thou savourest not the things that be of God, but
> those that be of men" (Mt. 16:22,23).

It seems to me that right here we have found a key—if not *the* key—to exactly what Satan really is. Just before this exchange Jesus had praised Peter for revealing his understanding—from the Holy Spirit—that He was ". . . the Christ, the Son of the living God" (Mt. 16:16). Now, after Peter rebukes Him and tells Him he is not going to let God's plan proceed, Jesus tells him he is Satan because he "savourest not the things that be of God, but those that be of men." Was Jesus saying that Peter was literally Satan? Not hardly. Peter was expressing rebellion against God. At that point he was expressing the spirit of rebellion, symbolically called Satan by Christ. Some say that Jesus was speaking to Satan who was standing behind Peter but the scripture says Jesus was speaking to Peter. At another time Jesus said; "Have not I chosen you twelve and one of you is a devil? He spake of Judas Iscariot..." (John 6:70,71). Later, we are told that Satan entered Judas, indicating that he had determined to betray Jesus (John 13:27). How is it that a serpent—that has been cursed by God to crawl on his belly eating dust for the rest of his days—enter into Judas?

The armor of God

Paul uses symbolism in describing how a Christian should be protected against the attack of the wicked:

> "Finally, my brethren, be strong in the Lord, and in the power of his might. Put on the whole armour of God, that ye may be able to stand against the wiles of the devil. For we wrestle not against flesh and blood, but against principalities, against powers, against the rulers of the darkness of this world, against spiritual wickedness in high *places*. Wherefore take unto you the whole armour of God, that ye may be able to withstand in the evil day, and having done all, to stand. Stand therefore, having your loins girt about with truth, and having on the breastplate of righteousness; And your feet shod with the preparation of the gospel of peace; Above all, taking the shield of faith, wherewith ye shall be able to quench all the fiery darts of the wicked. And take the helmet of salvation, and the sword of the Spirit, which is the word of God" (Eph. 6:10-17).

Paul mentions armor, which includes a helmet, a breastplate, a shield, a sword, etc. The wicked in this passage are presumed by most to be Satan and his demons that attack the Lord's saints with fiery darts. Since the armor and the fiery darts are symbolic, isn't it also reasonable to assume that Satan and his demons are symbolic in this context?

What about the 40 days?

In light of the above, I believe that references to Satan or the devil in Scripture are really references to rebellious, unredeemed human nature. The story of the temptations of Jesus in the wilderness is no exception. Jesus was beginning His commission. He had just been baptized, after which He went into the desert and fasted forty days. After the forty days the devil tempted Him (Mt. 4:1-11).

When Jesus incarnated in the flesh, He took on all the attributes of human nature (Phil. 2:7). I believe that before Jesus could begin His ministry He had to struggle with and totally overcome His own adopted physical human nature. His temptations are the story of that struggle and victory. For example:

> ➢ "For in that he himself hath suffered being tempted, he is able to succour them that are tempted" (Heb. 2:18).

> ➢ "For we have not an high priest which cannot be touched with the feeling of our infirmities; but was in all points tempted like as we are, yet without sin" (Heb. 4:15).

References to the devil are used to personify His human nature, as I believe they are used throughout Scripture. Also I wonder if this wilderness struggle is what is being referred to in Hebrews 5:8,9: "Though He were a Son, yet learned He obedience by the things which He suffered. And being made perfect, He became the author of eternal salvation unto all them that obey Him." By the way, notice that last sentence states only those who *obey* Jesus will receive eternal salvation. I'll go into more detail on that later.

Lucifer

The popular belief is that Satan began as an angel named Lucifer who was so well thought of in Heaven that he had a higher position than anyone except Christ Himself. Lucifer was always in the very presence of God. Then, one day he began to think he was better than God and that his way was better than God's way. He persuaded a third of the other angels to join him in his rebellion to try to replace God so that he could sit on God's throne and rule creation in God's place. His rebellion failed, his name was changed to Satan and he and his followers were thrown out of Heaven to earth where they continued their rebellion by persuading humans to disobey God.

If Lucifer was an angel with the highest position in Heaven, he must have known God better than anyone except Christ and the Holy Spirit. He also must have been extremely intelligent. So how does this super intelligent angel residing in the very presence of God for God knows how long, conceive of the notion that his way is better than God's way and that he can replace God on His throne? And then, having decided on this course of action, how could he have persuaded a third of the angels to follow him, assuming the other angels also knew God intimately and were also super intelligent? And then after having proceeded with his plan, being defeated in battle and thrown out of Heaven down to earth along with his followers, he and they continued to defy God and His plan here on earth down to the present time! None of this makes any sense to me. What is in it for Satan and his followers? Surely they must realize they can't possibly win. What do they stand to gain by persuading humans to disobey God?

CHAPTER FOUR

THE GARDEN OF EDEN

I believe the story of the Garden of Eden is a parable or allegory. If we accept the story of the Garden of Eden as literal we are faced with several problems. One is the fact that on the sixth day of creation week it is revealed that God created man male and female (Gen. 1:27). That would mean Adam and Eve were both created in one day. But according to the Eden story God first made Adam, then He had him name all the cattle, the fowl of the air and every beast of the field. Did he do all that in one day? Then finally God made Eve from Adam's rib.

Another problem with a literal interpretation is we are told about two special trees that have special powers; the tree of life, and the tree of the knowledge of good and evil. Both of these trees have fruit that impart special powers. One imparts eternal life and the other special knowledge. Also, there is a special talking snake in this garden that is later identified as Satan (Rev. 9:12; 20:2). Nowhere else in all of Scripture is there any suggestion that eternal life or knowledge can be transmitted by eating magic fruit. On the contrary, in the case of eternal life, we are told throughout Scripture that we must repent of our sins and submit to God (Jesus Christ) as Lord. Scripture consistently teaches that forgiveness always follows repentance. For example:

> ➤ "Therefore I will judge you, O house of Israel, every one according to his ways, saith the Lord

GOD. Repent, and turn *yourselves* from all your transgressions; so iniquity shall not be your ruin. (Ezek. 18:30).

➢ ". . . the Kingdom of God is at hand, repent ye, and believe the gospel" (Mk. 1:15).

➢ "...except ye repent, ye shall all likewise perish" (Lk. 13:3,5).

➢ "Repent, and be baptized every one of you in the name of Jesus Christ for the remission of sins, and ye shall receive the gift of the Holy Ghost" (Acts 2:38).

➢ "Repent ye therefore, and be converted, that your sins may be blotted out" (Acts 3:19).

The symbolism of man's origin

If we accept the story of the Garden of Eden as literal, then we will have to say the scriptures contradict in the most important doctrine—salvation! Eternal life is attained through Christ, not by eating magic fruit from a magic tree. Neither is knowledge gained by eating magic fruit. Rather we attain knowledge by experience and study. Knowledge that cannot be attained in these ways can be attained by revelation. God has revealed knowledge about Himself, beginnings, our nature, our need for salvation and His plan for our salvation. None of this knowledge can be gained by eating fruit from a tree. Therefore, I believe the Garden of Eden story is an allegory containing symbols. I believe it is the symbolic story of the beginning of the human condition and our fall after Genesis 1:1.

I believe that before the beginning only God existed in the three persons of the Trinity: Father, Son, and Holy Spirit. There are some who doubt that the Holy Spirit is a person. Ephesians 4:30 convinces me He is: "And grieve not the holy Spirit of God." It seems to me that we cannot grieve a principle or idea, but we can grieve a person. Also:

"Howbeit when He, the Spirit of truth is come, He will guide you into all truth, for He shall not speak of Himself, but whatsoever He shall hear, that shall He speak, and He will show you things to come. He shall glorify Me, for He shall receive of Mine and shall show it unto you" (John 16:13,14).

Not only is the Holy Spirit spoken of here as "He," but He is doing things: guiding, speaking, hearing, showing, glorifying and receiving. Are these not the attributes of a person? He also indwells the saints, which He could not do unless He had the Divine attribute of omnipresence.

God the Son created the universe and the angels (John 1:1-3). I believe this is the story of Eden and its first inhabitants. The angels were created in the image of God. God is Spirit (John 4:24) and the angels were spirit. God has a mind and the angels had a mind. God has free will and the angels had free will.

The creation of the angels

God's purpose for creating the angels was for companionship:

> ➤ "And the scripture was fulfilled which saith, Abraham believed God, and it was imputed unto him for righteousness: and he was called the Friend of God" (Jas. 2:23).

> ➤ ". . . for Thou hast created all things, and for Thy pleasure they are and were created" (Rev. 4:11).

In order to have companions He had to give the angels free will. In giving them free will He had to refrain from forcing His will on them. He could not create character in the angels without violating their free will and thus defeating the very purpose for their creation—companionship. They had to develop character through the things they experienced and the choices they made. He could not build in obedience without interfering with their free will. They had to be companions with Him because that was their choice. Forced companionship is not true companionship. He could not force them to love Him. He could not force them to want to obey Him. Love and obedience had to develop in each individual through experience with Him.

In order for God to create the universe He had to establish certain laws. The physical laws that hold the creation together are based on spiritual laws. Breaking these laws is sin and results in death. These principles were taught to the angels, but truth is never really known unless it is experienced. I can hear about the pain of hunger, but until I experience hunger I will never really know that pain. The angels were taught the correct way to live. They were taught the difference between right and wrong. They were taught that sin is the transgression of the law (1 John 3:4) and the wages of sin is death (Rom. 6:23), but since they had never experienced death they did not know what death was.

Rebellion

The angels began to go throughout creation experiencing, growing and developing character. This is the symbolism of Adam and Eve in the Garden of Eden. They had direct access to eternal life represented by the tree of life. By living in obedience to God they would have life but disobedience would bring separation and death. All they had to do was choose good and avoid evil as God defined those terms. Some of the angels began to follow a course that was contrary to God's will. They decided they could define good and evil. This is the symbology of eating the forbidden fruit. Instead of relying on God's definition of good and evil they chose to ignore Him and make that decision for themselves. As they moved in this direction they began to drift farther and farther away from the good that God had revealed to them. They were following a path that seemed good to them but was in opposition to what God had revealed was good. "There is a way which seemeth right unto a man, but the end thereof are the ways of death" (Pr. 14:12; 16:25). More and more they were following the spirit of rebellion. They were accusing God of being in error. They thought they were right and God was wrong. This spirit of rebellion and accusation is the definition of Satan, in my opinion.

Separation

In the beginning of the Eden story, we are told that Adam was
made from the dust of the ground. This sounds like the earth, but
if the story is symbolic then certain earth symbols can be used
symbolically. We are also told that God formed Eve from one of
Adam's ribs. I believe that when God first created the angels He
created them without defining sexual attributes as Jesus suggested.
Perhaps each angel possessed the spiritual equivalent of both male
and female attributes in perfect balance. When God began His plan
of salvation on earth He accentuated the male attribute in some and
the female in others. The story of Eve coming from Adam's rib
is the story of this separation. Each individual still contains both
sexual attributes, but in the male the female attribute is suppressed,
and in the female the male attribute is suppressed. This is not found
in Scripture in such detail, but Edgar Cayce (more about him later)
made this claim in some of his readings and it makes sense to me.
Jesus does seem to suggest this when He said:

> "For in the resurrection they neither marry, nor
> are given in marriage, but are as the angels of God in
> heaven" (Mt. 22:30).

God could not allow these angels to continue their disobedience
throughout His creation. As a matter of fact, they had separated
themselves from God—the "Tree of Life"—and were now under
the death penalty as the law demanded. Since God is just He had
every right to execute sentence against these rebellious angels
immediately, but God is also merciful:

> "And the LORD passed by before him [Moses], and
> proclaimed, The LORD, the LORD God, merciful and
> gracious, longsuffering, and abundant in goodness and
> truth, keeping mercy for thousands, forgiving iniquity
> and transgression and sin..." (Ex. 34:6,7).

The angels' rebellion did not take God by surprise. Since He had given His angels free will, He did not know exactly what choices they would make, but He did know all the choices that were possible, including rebellion. It is not that God does not know everything there is to know about everyone and everything, but in His sovereignty He can choose to limit Himself. So He already had a plan ready in the event that path was chosen:

> "Forasmuch as ye know that ye were not redeemed with corruptible things, as silver and gold, from your vain conversation [manner of life] received by tradition from your fathers, but with the precious blood of Christ, as of a lamb without blemish and without spot, who verily was foreordained before the foundation of the world, but was manifest in these last times for you" (1 Pet. 1:18-20).

Since death was the penalty for sin, that penalty could not be changed without destroying the law and bringing down all of creation, since creation depends on God's law for its existence. But the angels could be saved from death if someone died in their place. Someone else had to receive their punishment for them. There was only one person in all of creation who could do such a thing and that was God Himself, the one who had created everything and everyone in the first place and had established the laws that made it all work. But just paying their penalty for them would not bring about repentance on the part of the disobedient angels. First, they had to understand that their way was wrong and God's way was right—and repent.

When the angels rebelled, they were making a statement. They were saying that God's revelation of good and evil was incorrect and they took on themselves to define what was good and evil. This is the symbol of the tree of the knowledge of good and evil in the Garden of Eden. When they began to decide for themselves what was good and evil they were eating forbidden fruit. They were saying their way was better than God's revealed way. That attitude persists to this day among most of the people on earth, doesn't it?

Judgment

About a third of the angels made this statement and the rest of them knew of it. If God had destroyed the rebellious angels at that point His righteousness and power would have been demonstrated and the surviving angels would have served God more out of fear than love, which was not God's desire. Also the question would remain unanswered: was God's way really right? Would the path the rebellious angels had taken really have ended in disaster? These questions would have remained unanswered if God had exercised His righteousness and destroyed them. Besides, God is merciful and did not want to lose a single angel. As we are told in 2 Peter 3:9; "The Lord is not slack concerning his promise, as some men count slackness, but is longsuffering to us-ward [toward us], not willing that any should perish, but that all should come to repentance." God is life, not death.

Death and destruction are not part of God's nature although He will resort to such measures if necessary, after all else fails. We have a sober reminder of this fact in Isaiah 28:21; "For the LORD shall rise up as in mount Perazim. He shall be wroth as in the valley of Gibeon, that He may do His work, His strange work, and bring to pass His act, His strange act." In Deuteronomy 30:19,20, God seems to be pleading as He says; "I call heaven and earth to record this day against you, that I have set before you life and death, blessing and cursing. Therefore choose life, that both thou and thy seed may live, that thou mayest love the LORD thy God, and that thou mayest obey His voice, and that thou mayest cleave unto Him, for He is thy life, and the length of thy days..." Jesus expressed the same feeling in Matthew 23:37 when He said:

> "O Jerusalem, Jerusalem, thou that killest the prophets, and stonest them which are sent unto thee. How often would I have gathered thy children together, even as a hen gathereth her chickens under her wings, and ye would not!"

Can you hear the sobs in these statements? Down through history to this present time we witness mankind's tendency to choose death instead of life, don't we? The worldwide practice of murdering unborn babies is just one example. In the United States alone over 3000 babies are legally murdered every day, and most of us ignore and/or accept this fact.

Incidentally, Jesus could not have made such a statement were He not God. So we have here more evidence of Jesus' divinity. Also notice that God is always leaving up to us the choice of whether or not we will obey Him. We may not decide what is right and wrong as in situation ethics. We must choose to obey the morality God has established and revealed—or die. "Sin is the transgression of the law" (1 John 3:4), and "the wages of sin is death" (Rom. 6:23).

Confined to Earth

And so God confined the rebellious angels to earth. When the disobedient angels arrived, they were furious at having their wings clipped, so to speak. They had literally been grabbed by the scruff of their necks and yanked out of their freewheeling roaming throughout God's creation and confined to this tiny speck of dust called earth. I believe this is vividly and symbolically portrayed in Revelation 12:7-12.

They had never before experienced restraint and they reacted like spoiled brats that have just been told they can't have the moon. It may be noticed that the above passage from Revelation goes on to say; "And when the dragon saw that he was cast unto the earth, he persecuted the woman which brought forth the man *child...*" (v. 13). It may be objected that the rest of this passage does not fit my analogy very well and admittedly it doesn't unless we consider the fact that this is highly symbolical and the time between verse 12 and 13 is not necessarily immediate.

Destruction

I believe that even though they could no longer roam freely throughout creation, they still retained some of their angelic powers. Giving full vent to their rage they literally raised hell here on earth to such an extent that they destroyed it. Volcanic dust and debris in the atmosphere was miles thick, cutting out all light. Genesis 1:2 describes the scene this way: "And the earth was without form, and void, and darkness was upon the face of the deep." The word "was" in this verse is translated from the Hebrew word "hayah" which can also be translated "became" and has been in over 65 Bible verses from Genesis 2:7 through Ezekiel 36:4. Some examples are:

> "...and man **became** a living soul...And a river went out of Eden to water the garden; and from thence it was parted, and **became** into four heads...But his wife looked back from behind him, and she **became** a pillar of salt...which **became** a prey and derision to the residue of the heathen that *are* round about" (Gen. 2:7,10; 19:26; Ezek. 36:4).

After the disobedient angels had destroyed the earth with their tantrum, there was no more they could do. They had literally reached the end of their rope. Jesus may have had this period in mind in His parable of the prodigal son, when he reached the point where he was starving in the pigpen (Lk. 15:11-16). God allowed these angels to demonstrate to themselves as well as the other angels what happens when they go their own way outside of His will.

Renewal

I believe that when man first appeared on earth, he appeared in five different places as the five races. In Genesis 1:26,27 we learn:

> "And God said, Let Us make man in Our image, after Our likeness, and let them have dominion over the fish of the sea, and over the fowl of the air, and over the cattle, and over all the earth, and over every creeping thing that creepeth upon the earth. So God created man in His own image, in the image of God created He him; male and female created He them."

The word "man" in this passage comes from the Hebrew word "adam," and means a human being, an individual or mankind. I believe the context here calls for the translation "mankind."

Also, up to this point He said, "Let there be light . . . a firmament . . . let the earth bring forth grass . . . the fruit tree..." etc. But when He created mankind He said "Let Us make man in Our image..." God seems to be saying here that mankind is totally different from the rest of His creation.

Incest

Much of this is speculation on my part, but if God did create all of mankind on the earth at the same time as Genesis 1:26,27 seems to teach; it explains where Cain's wife came from, as well as the different races. The law, as given to Moses, included the prohibition against incest. Of course we know that Adam came before Moses but I believe the law existed before the beginning and was taught to Adam and Eve (mankind). I'll go into more detail about that later. Since God never changes, as He declares in Scripture, then it is unlikely He would approve of the descendents of Adam and Eve committing incest. There seems to be an exception to this in the story of Abraham and Sarah. Abraham described Sarah, his wife, as his sister on two different occasions for the same reason; he was afraid the king of the country he was in would want her as his wife and would kill him for her because she was so beautiful. The first time this happened, they were in Egypt (Gen. 12:11-19). The next time this happened, they were in the country of Gerar and Abimelech was the king. Abraham hadn't learned anything in Egypt evidently because he did the same thing (Gen. 20:2-13).

Abraham was obviously no more perfect than any of us, was he? And yet God chose him to be the father of His "chosen people." Not only was Abraham a liar, but also he was committing incest with his sister. Sometimes all we can do is accept Romans 11:33-36:

> "O the depth of the riches both of the wisdom
> and knowledge of God! How unsearchable are His
> judgments, and His ways past finding out! For who

hath known the mind of the Lord, or who hath been
His counsellor? Or who hath first given to Him, and it
shall be recompensed unto Him again? For of Him, and
through Him, and to Him, are all things, to whom be
glory for ever. Amen."

Perhaps this is an example of God's mercy. It is certainly an
example of His sovereignty, isn't it? He doesn't always reveal His
reason for the things He does, He just does them. If we remember
the above passage in Romans, we can more readily accept His will,
even though we don't always understand why. We can remember
also that He loves us; "For God so loved the world, that He gave
His only begotten Son, that whosoever believeth in Him should not
perish, but have everlasting life" (John 3:16), and He will never
leave us nor forsake us (Heb. 13:5).

Abraham came from a tribe of people who were pagan idol
worshippers. When God called him he was already married to
Sarah in accordance with the customs of his people. He didn't
know everything there is to know about God, but then who does?
He was probably a very religious man and was teachable. This, I
think, is a very important trait that we would all do well to develop.
When we think we have the truth, the whole truth, and nothing
but the truth, and there is no possibility we could be mistaken, we
aren't teachable and probably wouldn't recognize the truth if it
came up and poked us in the nose. After Abraham got into trouble
twice, lying about Sarah, God said: "Because that Abraham obeyed
My voice, and kept My charge, My commandments, My statutes,
and My laws" (Gen. 26:5). It sounds like Abraham was a good
student even though he was 75 years old when God called him.
So just because God used and blessed Abraham does not mean he
approved of his sins. This is a good example of God's love, grace
and forgiveness toward those who learn His truth and apply it.

The fall

In affect God told His fallen angels, "You say your way is better
than My way. All right, we will see. I am giving you the world and
all the raw material you need to experiment with your way. With

your intelligence you have everything you need to create paradise or hell. We shall see how much better your way is." And so human history began on earth and mankind was given the physical version of the spiritual law that holds creation together—The Ten Commandments.

One objection I have heard concerning the idea that life existed on earth before Adam is a reference to 1 Corinthians 15:22 which says, "For as in Adam all die, even so in Christ shall all be made alive." Romans 5:12 expresses the same thought. The reasoning here seems to be that if all died as a result of Adam's sin, then there was no death before Adam, and therefore there could have been no plants and animals dying before Adam. I believe the verse refers to mankind only, not to blood cells, germs, insects, etc. Otherwise nothing could eat anything since something always dies when it is eaten. Think about it: If insects never died how long would it take for the world to be so full of them we wouldn't be able to move. Also, I believe this verse is referring to Adam in the sense of mankind first sinning when we were still angels before we were confined to earth in material bodies. Scripture does say; "And Adam called his wife's name Eve; because she was the mother of all living" (Gen. 3:20). This seems to conflict with the idea that mankind was created by God before Adam and Eve. I believe God created physical bodies for the fallen angels so they could express themselves in a physical three-dimensional world, as is revealed in Genesis 1:26,27.

After the angels had their tantrum on earth they were the spiritual equivalent of someone who has been terribly burned in a fire, or someone who has been severely injured in an accident. God's six days of creation were spent re-creating the earth. On the sixth day He re-created (healed) His fallen angels in His image: mind, spirit, and will; but this time adding the physical equivalent of His image, providing a physical vehicle through which they could express themselves in a physical, three dimensional world.

God then inserts a parable in a parenthesis in Genesis two and three giving a symbolic review of man's beginning and fall and using two real people, Adam and Eve, on whom He focuses in the rest of Scripture. It is from these two that the chosen people came. This race was the vehicle for the writing of Scripture, which records for mankind God's nature, our nature, our need for salvation, His plan of salvation and the history of His relationship with His chosen people and their neighbors. After the flood all wicked mankind was destroyed except the descendents of Adam and Eve through Noah and his family. Thus Eve is indeed the "mother of all living" since the wicked perished in the flood.

Romans 5:19 says: "For as by one man's disobedience many were made sinners, so by the obedience of one shall many be made righteous." This verse seems to contradict the idea that the sin of Adam and Eve was actually symbolic of the story of spiritual mankind's rebellion against God as outlined above. I believe the symbology is still valid. The man (Adam) in the verse can still be considered symbolic of mankind without changing the meaning.

CHAPTER FIVE

THE LAW

Even though the Bible does not formally lay out the law until Exodus 20 when God writes the Ten Commandments with His finger on two stone tablets and gives them to Moses (Ex. 31:18; Dt. 9:10), it is clear to me that the law existed before that event. The first hint that the law was known earlier is in Genesis 4:6,7: "And the LORD said unto Cain, Why art thou wroth, and why is thy countenance fallen? If thou doest well, shalt thou not be accepted? And if thou doest not well, sin lieth at the door." In 1 John 3:4, we learn that ". . . sin is the transgression of the law." In Romans 4:15 we learn that ". . . where no law is, there is no transgression." Since sin is the transgression of the law, then Cain could not have sinned if there had been no law at that time which said, "Thou shalt not kill." The Hebrew word translated "kill" here is ratsach, and means murder. Some people think the commandment not to kill means we can't kill anything. If that were true, then God contradicted Himself because in Exodus 12:6,21 He said; "And ye shall keep it up until the fourteenth day of the same month: and the whole assembly of the congregation of Israel shall kill it in the evening . . . Then Moses called for all the elders of Israel, and said unto them, Draw out and take you a lamb according to your families, and kill the passover." The word "kill" in this passage is translated from the Hebrew word shachat which means to slaughter, and is found in many other verses such as Exodus 29:11,20 which have to do with killing animals for sacrifice, which God commanded. He also commanded murderers to be killed.

The Law before Moses

As I mentioned earlier, Abraham told King Abimelech that Sarah, his wife, was his sister. Abimelech took Sarah with the intention of making her his wife, but God warned him in a dream that he was about to commit the sin of adultery. Abimelech objected that he was deceived and did this in the integrity of his heart and innocence of his hands. Then God said to him in a dream, "Yea, I know that thou didst this in the integrity of thy heart, for I also withheld thee from sinning against Me." (Gen. 20:6).

In Genesis 26:5 we read: "Because that Abraham obeyed My voice, and kept My charge, My commandments, My statutes, and My laws." In Genesis 39:9 Joseph is talking to Potiphar's wife who is trying to get Joseph to sleep with her in her husband's absence. Joseph said, "There is none greater in this house than I. Neither hath he kept back any thing from me but thee, because thou art his wife. How then can I do this great wickedness, and sin against God?" These examples are pretty good evidence that the Ten Commandments were well known even among aliens, before Moses formally received them on the two stone tablets written with God's finger. In each case sin—the transgression of God's Ten Commandment Law (1 John 3:4)—is condemned.

God's kingdom and the Law

God was establishing a kingdom over the Israelites with Himself as the King. Earlier He had come in person at Mount Sinai and through Moses had made an offer to the people that if "ye will obey My voice indeed, and keep My covenant, then ye shall be a peculiar treasure unto Me above all people. For all the earth is Mine . . . And ye shall be unto Me a kingdom of priests, and an holy nation. These are the words which thou shalt speak unto the children of Israel . . . And all the people answered together, and said, All that the LORD hath spoken we will do. And Moses returned the words of the people unto the LORD" (Ex. 19:5,6,8).

So the people agreed to accept God as their King and it was only after this that God formally gave Moses the Ten Commandments on the stone tablets.

In reading the scriptures I constantly come across passages declaring the law to be the central issue. Obedience brings blessings and disobedience brings suffering and death. Consider the following:

> ➤ "O that there were such an heart in them, that they would fear Me, and keep all My Commandments always, that it might be well with them, and with their children for ever!" (Dt. 5:29).

> ➤ "The law of the LORD is perfect, converting the soul" (Ps. 19:7).

> ➤ ". . . all His Commandments are sure. They stand fast for ever and ever, and are done in truth and uprightness" (Ps. 111:7,8).

> ➤ "Blessed is the man that feareth the LORD, that delighteth greatly in His Commandments" (Ps. 112:1).

> ➤ "And I will execute vengeance in anger and wrath on the nations which have not obeyed" (Micah 5:15 NASB).

> ➤ "Think not that I am come to destroy the law, or the prophets. I am not come to destroy, but to fulfil. For verily I say unto you, Till heaven and earth pass, one jot or one tittle shall in no wise pass from the law, till all be fulfilled. Whosoever therefore shall break one of these least Commandments, and shall teach men so, he shall be called the least in the Kingdom of Heaven. But whosoever shall do and teach them, the same shall be called great in the Kingdom of Heaven" (Mt. 5:17-19).

> ➤ "Not every one that saith unto Me, Lord, Lord, shall enter into the Kingdom of Heaven, but he that doeth the will of My Father which is in heaven" (Mt. 7:21).

> ➤ ". . . if thou wilt enter into life, keep the commandments" (Mt. 19:17).

> ➤ "Circumcision is nothing, and uncircumcision is nothing, but the keeping of the commandments of God" (1 Cor. 7:19).

> ➤ "...he that doeth the will of God abideth for ever" (1 John 2:17).

There are many more, but these verses should be sufficient to show how very important is obedience to God's Ten Commandment Law. Also, consider the following:

GOD IS		**HIS LAW IS**	
Righteous	Ezra 9:15	Righteous	Ps. 119:172
Perfect	Mt. 5:48	Perfect	Ps. 19:7
Holy	Lev. 19:2	Holy	Rom. 7:12
Good	Ps. 34:8	Good	Rom. 7:12
Truth	Dt. 32:4	Truth	Ps. 119:142
Eternal	Dt. 33:27	Eternal	Ps. 111:7,8
Light	John 8:12	Light	Pr. 6:23

The Law and salvation

I have been assured many times that the Ten Commandment Law has absolutely nothing to do with salvation. That salvation is freely given only after we believe that Jesus is our savior and we only obey God after we are saved out of love and gratitude for His gift of salvation. When I notice that most believers disobey God by refusing to keep holy His Sabbath day, it seems these believers aren't saved by their own admission. I agree that salvation cannot be earned, and it is a gift, but I also believe we have to meet God's requirements or conditions before we can receive that gift. I believe that belief is only one of four steps toward salvation. These steps are:

> ➤ To hear the truth
> ➤ To understand the truth
> ➤ To believe the truth
> ➤ To apply the truth

Most people do not even hear the truth. Instead, they hear a counterfeit. So they do not even get past step one.

Many who believe obeying God's Ten Commandment Law has nothing to do with eternal life tend to either ignore or twist the words of Jesus in Matthew 7:21-23:

> "Not every one that saith unto me, Lord, Lord, shall enter into the kingdom of heaven; but he that doeth the will of my Father which is in heaven. Many will say to me in that day, Lord, Lord, have we not prophesied in thy name? and in thy name have cast out devils? and in thy name done many wonderful works? And then will I profess unto them, I never knew you: depart from me, ye that work iniquity."

Iniquity means lawlessness. The New American Standard Bible translates that last verse this way: "And then I will declare to them, 'I never knew you; DEPART FROM ME, YOU WHO PRACTICE LAWLESSNESS.'" The NASB is considered by most scholars to be the most accurate and literal translation available today.

So Jesus is saying that not everyone who just believes in Him will enter the kingdom of heaven but only those who not only believe in Him but also obey His Father's Ten Commandment Law. If people call Him Lord, Lord, they must believe in Him, right? If they practice lawlessness, then they are disobeying His Father's Ten Commandment Law, according to His definition, and that is the only moral Law I know of that is associated with the Father.

The ceremonial law, which consisted of animal sacrifices, etc., was about to come to and end at the cross.

I hear a great deal about salvation being based on faith and faith only. When I search the scriptures I find that the phrase "faith only" or "faith alone" is only found one time in James 2:24: "Ye see then how that by works a man is justified, and not by faith only." James seems to be saying that we are justified (saved) by works, not by faith. That really flies in the face of the "faith only" idea, doesn't it? Was James teaching that we must work our way into heaven? Not hardly! He was simply pointing out that "faith without works is dead" (vs. 26). Let's take a look at the context:

> "What *doth it* profit, my brethren, though a man say he hath faith, and have not works? can faith save him? If a brother or sister be naked, and destitute of daily food, And one of you say unto them, Depart in peace, be *ye* warmed and filled; notwithstanding ye give them not those things which are needful to the body; what *doth it* profit? Even so faith, if it hath not works, is dead, being alone. Yea, a man may say, Thou hast faith, and I have works: shew me thy faith without thy works, and I will shew thee my faith by my works. Thou believest that there is one God; thou doest well: the devils also believe, and tremble. But wilt thou know, O vain man, that faith without works is dead? Was not Abraham our father justified by works, when he had offered Isaac his son upon the altar? Seest thou how faith wrought with his works, and by works was faith made perfect? And the scripture was fulfilled which saith, Abraham believed God, and it was imputed unto him for righteousness: and he was called the Friend of God. Ye see then how that by works a man is justified, and not by faith only. Likewise also was not Rahab the harlot justified by works, when she had received the messengers, and had sent *them* out another way? For as the body without the spirit is dead, so faith without works is dead also" (Jas. 2:14-26).

I believe the Ten Commandment Law is at the very core of sin and salvation. God tells us: "Sin is the transgression of the law" (1 John 3:4), and ". . . the wages of sin is death, but the gift of God is eternal life through Jesus Christ our Lord" (Rom. 6:23). If we had not transgressed God's Ten Commandment Law (sinned) we would not have received the death penalty and there would have been no need for Jesus to shed His blood in our place.

And what is God's condition that we must meet before we can receive His gift of forgiveness and eternal life? Peter, under the influence of the Holy Spirit, was speaking to a crowd of about 3000 men on the day of Pentecost. He had just convinced them that they had committed the sin of murder because they had taken part in the crucifixion of Jesus their Messiah. Probably they had been part of the crowd that had yelled, "crucify him!" at Jesus' trial. "Now when they heard this, they were pricked in their heart, and said unto Peter and to the rest of the apostles, Men and brethren, what shall we do?" (Acts 2:37). Peter answered, "Repent, and be baptized every one of you in the name of Jesus Christ for the remission of sins, and ye shall receive the gift of the Holy Ghost" (Acts 2:38). Notice that repentance precedes forgiveness and the gift of the Holy Spirit. Romans 8:9 says: "But ye are not in the flesh, but in the Spirit, if so be that the Spirit of God dwell in you. Now if any man have not the Spirit of Christ, he is none of His." If we do not have the Spirit of Christ—the Holy Spirit—we do not belong to Christ, and we are not Christians, are we?

Notice that Peter did not answer the question by saying; "What do you have to do? Why, you don't have to *do* anything. Salvation is a gift. Now that you believe Jesus is your Messiah and died for your sins, that is all that is necessary. So cheer up. You now have eternal life and it can never be taken from you no matter what you think, say or do. You are saved forever. So go your way and enjoy life here and hereafter." Does that sound familiar? That idea seems to be the most popular notion making the rounds these days. If it is true, why didn't Peter say that instead of what he did say?

Moral vs. ceremonial law

Another notion making the rounds today is that the Law ended at the cross. In Ephesians 2:15 we find: "Having abolished in his flesh the enmity, *even* the law of commandments *contained* in ordinances..." On the surface, this verse does seem to teach that the law has been abolished. However, we need to remember there is a moral law and a ceremonial law. The moral law is the Ten Commandment Law and is described in Scripture as being perfect and eternal (Ps. 19:7; 111:7,8). It is never described as being contained in "ordinances." In Colossians 2:14 we find: "Blotting out the handwriting of ordinances that was against us, which was contrary to us, and took it out of the way, nailing it to his cross." This is often used to prove that the Ten Commandment Law was nailed to the cross, but if we read on we find this is referring to the ceremonial law: "Let no man therefore judge you in meat, or in drink, or in respect of an holyday, or of the new moon, or of the sabbath *days*: Which are a shadow of things to come; but the body *is* of Christ" (vv. 16,17). There were several annual Sabbath days that were part of the ceremonial law. This law had to do with animal sacrifices for the remission of sin and was a "shadow of things to come" pointing forward to the final sacrifice of Christ, the Lamb of God on the cross. These annual Sabbath days fell on different days of the week every year like our Christmas and Thanksgiving holidays. The weekly Sabbath is not a shadow the things to come but rather a reminder of the seventh day of creation week and the Creator of everything and everyone (Gen. 2:1-3; Ex. 20:11). Another more explicit example of the ceremonial law being referred to as a shadow is found in Hebrews 10:1-4:

> "For the law having a shadow of good things to come, *and* not the very image of the things, can never with those sacrifices which they offered year by year continually make the comers [those who draw near to worship] thereunto perfect. For then would they not have ceased to be offered? because that the worshippers once purged should have had no more conscience of sins. But in those *sacrifices there is* a remembrance again *made* of

sins every year. For *it is* not possible that the blood of bulls and of goats should take away sins."

Some examples of the difference between the two laws are:

> ➢ The Decalogue was spoken and written by God Himself (Ex. 20:1; 31:18; 32:16). The Ceremonial Law was spoken and written by Moses (Ex. 24:3,4; Dt. 31:9).

> ➢ Moses placed the Decalogue in the ark (Dt. 10:5). The Levites placed the ceremonial law by the side of the ark (Dt. 31:26).

> ➢ The Decalogue reveals sin (Rom. 7:7). The ceremonial law commands offerings for sin (Lev. 4:26,35).

> ➢ To transgress the Decalogue is sin (1 John 3:4). There is no sin attached to the ceremonial law (Eph. 2:15 see Rom. 4:15).

> ➢ If we transgress one commandment, we have transgressed the whole Decalogue (Jas. 2:10). The ceremonial law was no longer to be kept (Acts 15:24).

> ➢ The Decalogue is spiritual (Rom. 7:14). The ceremonial law is carnal (Heb. 7:16).

Is Christ the end of the law?

Occasionally someone quotes Romans 10:4 to prove Christ ended the Ten Commandment Law: "For Christ *is* the end of the law for righteousness to every one that believeth." If this means Christ terminated the Law, then Paul contradicted himself, because in Romans 3:31 he writes: "Do we then make void the law through faith? God forbid: yea, we establish the law." He also contradicts Jesus who said:

> "Think not that I am come to destroy the law, or the prophets: I am not come to destroy, but to fulfil For

verily I say unto you, Till heaven and earth pass, one jot
or one tittle shall in no wise pass from the law, till all be
fulfilled. Whosoever therefore shall break one of these
least commandments, and shall teach men so, he shall be
called the least in the kingdom of heaven: but whosoever
shall do and teach *them*, the same shall be called great in
the kingdom of heaven. For I say unto you, That except
your righteousness shall exceed *the righteousness* of the
scribes and Pharisees, ye shall in no case enter into the
kingdom of heaven" (Mt. 5:17-20).

If Christ was saying He came to end the law after saying He
did not come to destroy it, was He not contradicting Himself in
the same breath? We should be very cautious accepting the false
doctrine that the Law has been done away.

But the fact remains that Paul did say Christ is the end of the
Law. Admittedly, the word "end" can mean terminate. It can also
mean goal and I believe that is what the Spirit meant when He
inspired Paul to write that verse. So it should read Christ is the goal
or purpose of the Law, not the termination of the Law.

We would do well to remember what God said through Moses:
"And now, Israel, what doth the LORD thy God require of thee, but
to fear the LORD thy God, to walk in all his ways, and to love him,
and to serve the LORD thy God with all thy heart and with all thy
soul, To keep the commandments of the LORD, and his statutes,
which I command thee this day for thy good?" (Dt. 10:12,13).

Can we lose our salvation?

I believe our past sins are forgiven at repentance, but not our
future sins. Otherwise there would be no need for God—through
John—to tell Christians, "If we say that we have no sin, we deceive
ourselves, and the truth is not in us. If we confess our sins, He is
faithful and just to forgive us our sins, and to cleanse us from all
unrighteousness. If we say that we have not sinned, we make Him
a liar, and His word is not in us" (1 John 1:8-10). John is writing
here to Christians, and is telling them they will continue to sin,
and they must continue to seek forgiveness for their sins through

repentance. They must continue in an attitude of repentance. Most churches teach that once we are saved there is nothing we can think, say or do that will cause us to lose our salvation. The scripture I usually hear to support this belief is Romans 8:38,39: "For I am persuaded, that neither death, nor life, nor angels, nor principalities, nor powers, nor things present, nor things to come, nor height, nor depth, nor any other creature, shall be able to separate us from the love of God, which is in Christ Jesus our Lord." Notice that Paul uses the word "love," not "salvation." We know that "...God so loved the world, that He gave His only begotten Son, that whosoever believeth in Him should not perish, but have everlasting life" (John 3:16). God loves everyone. "But God commendeth His love toward us, in that, while we were yet sinners, Christ died for us" (Rom. 5:8). "For if, when we were enemies, we were reconciled to God by the death of His Son, much more, being reconciled, we shall be saved by His life" (Rom. 5:10).

Even though God loves everyone, He only gives eternal life to those who will repent of their sins, submit to Jesus Christ as LORD and obey His Ten Commandment Law. But once we have received salvation we can lose it if we choose to reject Christ and return to our former sinful life. We never lose our free will. Consider the following statements from God on this subject:

> ➢ "But if the wicked will turn from all his sins that he hath committed, and keep all My statutes, and do that which is lawful and right, he shall surely live, he shall not die. All his transgressions that he hath committed, they shall not be mentioned unto him. In his righteousness that he hath done he shall live. Have I any pleasure at all that the wicked should die saith the Lord GOD, and not that he should return from his ways, and live? But when the righteous turneth away from his righteousness, and committeth iniquity, and doeth according to all the abominations that the wicked man doeth, shall he live? All his righteousness that he hath done shall not be mentioned. In his trespass that he hath trespassed, and in his sin that he hath sinned, in

them shall he die...When the righteous turneth from his righteousness, and committeth iniquity, he shall even die thereby. But if the wicked turn from his wickedness, and do that which is lawful and right, he shall live thereby" (Ezek. 18:21-24; 33:18,19).

➤   "Therefore is the kingdom of heaven likened unto a certain king, which would take account of his servants. And when he had begun to reckon, one was brought unto him, which owed him ten thousand talents. But forasmuch as he had not to pay, his lord commanded him to be sold, and his wife, and children, and all that he had, and payment to be made. The servant therefore fell down, and worshipped him, saying, Lord, have patience with me, and I will pay thee all. Then the lord of that servant was moved with compassion, and loosed him, and forgave him the debt. But the same servant went out, and found one of his fellowservants, which owed him an hundred pence: and he laid hands on him, and took *him* by the throat, saying, Pay me that thou owest. And his fellowservant fell down at his feet, and besought him, saying, Have patience with me, and I will pay thee all. And he would not: but went and cast him into prison, till he should pay the debt. So when his fellowservants saw what was done, they were very sorry, and came and told unto their lord all that was done. Then his lord, after that he had called him, said unto him, O thou wicked servant, I forgave thee all that debt, because thou desiredst me: Shouldest not thou also have had compassion on thy fellowservant, even as I had pity on thee? And his lord was wroth, and delivered him to the tormentors, till he should pay all that was due unto him. So likewise shall my heavenly Father do also unto you, if ye from your hearts forgive not every one his brother their trespasses" (Mt. 18: 23-35).

The king in this parable forgives the servant for his debt as God forgives sinners. But notice that forgiveness was withdrawn when the servant continued in his sin. Here are a few more examples showing we can lose our salvation:

> ➤ "Every branch in me that beareth not fruit he taketh away…" (John 15:2).

> ➤ "For if the firstfruit *be* holy, the lump *is* also *holy*: and if the root *be* holy, so *are* the branches. And if some of the branches be broken off, and thou, being a wild olive tree, wert graffed [grafted] in among them, and with them partakest of the root and fatness of the olive tree; Boast not against the branches. But if thou boast, thou bearest not the root, but the root thee. Thou wilt say then, The branches were broken off, that I might be graffed in. Well; because of unbelief they were broken off, and thou standest by faith. Be not highminded, but fear: For if God spared not the natural branches, *take heed* lest he also spare not thee. Behold therefore the goodness and severity of God: on them which fell, severity; but toward thee, goodness, if thou continue in *his* goodness: otherwise thou also shalt be cut off. And they also, if they abide not still in unbelief, shall be graffed in: for God is able to graff them in again." (Rom. 11:16-23).

> ➤ "But I keep under my body, and bring *it* into subjection: lest that by any means, when I have preached to others, I myself should be a castaway" (1 Cor. 9:27).

> ➤ "And you, that were sometime alienated and enemies in *your* mind by wicked works, yet now hath he reconciled In the body of his flesh through death, to present you holy and unblameable and unreproveable in his sight: If ye continue in the faith grounded and

settled, and *be* not moved away from the hope of the gospel, which ye have heard..." (Col. 1:21-23).

➤ If we suffer, we shall also reign with *him*: if we deny *him*, he also will deny us" (2 Tim. 2:12).

➤ "Take heed, brethren, lest there be in any of you an evil heart of unbelief, in departing from the living God. But exhort one another daily, while it is called To day; lest any of you be hardened through the deceitfulness of sin. For we are made partakers of Christ, if we hold the beginning of our confidence stedfast unto the end" (Heb. 3:12-14).

➤ "For *it is* impossible for those who were once enlightened, and have tasted of the heavenly gift, and were made partakers of the Holy Ghost, And have tasted the good word of God, and the powers of the world to come, If they shall fall away, to renew them again unto repentance; seeing they crucify to themselves the Son of God afresh, and put *him* to an open shame" (Heb. 6:4-6).

➤ "For if we sin wilfully after that we have received the knowledge of the truth, there remaineth no more sacrifice for sins, But a certain fearful looking for of judgment and fiery indignation, which shall devour the adversaries. He that despised Moses' law died without mercy under two or three witnesses: Of how much sorer punishment, suppose ye, shall he be thought worthy, who hath trodden under foot the Son of God, and hath counted the blood of the covenant, wherewith he was sanctified, an unholy thing, and hath done despite unto the Spirit of grace?" (Heb. 10:26-29).

➤ "Remember therefore from whence thou art fallen, and repent, and do the first works; or else I will come unto thee quickly, and will remove thy candlestick out of his place, except thou repent" (Rev. 2:5).

Those who do not wish to believe we can lose our salvation deny that any of the above verses teach that we can, but it sure looks that way to me. In Hebrews 6:4-6 and 10:26-29 it looks like we are being told that if we do lose our salvation there is no further hope for us. This is not what is being taught. What God is saying is that Jesus died for our sins once and doesn't need to do it again. He is our only hope of salvation and that hope remains open to all who will repent:

> ➤ "If we confess our sins, he is faithful and just to forgive us *our* sins, and to cleanse us from all unrighteousness" (1 John 1:9).

> ➤ "My little children, these things write I unto you, that ye sin not. And if any man sin, we have an advocate with the Father, Jesus Christ the righteous: And he is the propitiation for our sins: and not for ours only, but also for the sins of the whole world. And hereby we do know that we know him, if we keep his commandments. He that saith, I know him, and keepeth not his commandments, is a liar, and the truth is not in him (1 John 2:1-4).

By the way, isn't it interesting that John refers to Jesus as the Father? Is this another hint of the trinity?

Are we born knowing right from wrong?

Occasionally I am assured that everyone is born knowing the difference between right and wrong. It seems to me that God disagrees with that belief. For example:

> "The wicked are estranged from the womb: they go astray as soon as they be born, speaking lies" (Ps. 58:3).

Surly all parents can testify that their children do not need to be taught to lie; it just comes naturally. I think of cultures that believe there is nothing wrong with eating enemies, cutting off people's heads and shrinking them, killing six million Jews, killing all men, women and children who don't believe in Islam, etc. In God's Ten Commandment Law He reveals what is right and wrong. Most of the commandments appear in other religions and civil codes in one form or another because no matter how primitive a culture may be they figure out that in order to live together in peace they must refrain from certain behavior such as stealing, murder, etc. The Sabbath commandment is a glaring universal exception. Is anyone born knowing he should keep God's Sabbath day holy? I have heard lawyers claim that right and wrong is determined by the laws of their locale or nation. These concepts of right and wrong are based on human ideas and are subject to change at any time. They are not absolute values. I believe this is our basic problem. In the beginning God revealed to us what is right and good. We chose to ignore God's revelation and decide for ourselves what is right and good and we are still making that fatal error. That is the symbology of the tree of the knowledge of good and evil in the Garden of Eden. We will continue to reap the consequences of our error until we repent of our sins, submit to Jesus Christ as LORD and obey His Ten Commandment Law.

Covenants

There are some who claim God's Ten Commandment Law is confined to the Old Covenant. Scripture doesn't seem to support that idea. The first mention of a covenant in Scripture is found in Genesis 6:18: "But with thee will I establish My covenant; and thou shalt come into the ark, thou, and thy sons, and thy wife, and thy sons' wives with thee." God is telling Noah He *will* establish His covenant, but He doesn't say at this time what it is. In Genesis 9:9-13, after the flood, He says:

> "And I, behold, I establish My covenant with you, and
> with your seed after you; and with every living creature that
> is with you, of the fowl, of the cattle, and of every beast
> of the earth with you; from all that go out of the ark, to
> every beast of the earth. And I will establish My covenant
> with you; neither shall all flesh be cut off any more by the
> waters of a flood; neither shall there any more be a flood

to destroy the earth. And God said, This is the token of the covenant which I make between Me and you and every living creature that is with you, for perpetual generations: I do set my bow in the cloud, and it shall be for a token of a covenant between Me and the earth. And it shall come to pass, when I bring a cloud over the earth, that the bow shall be seen in the cloud, and I will remember My covenant, which is between Me and you and every living creature of all flesh; and the waters shall no more become a flood to destroy all flesh. And the bow shall be in the cloud; and I will look upon it, that I may remember the everlasting covenant between God and every living creature of all flesh that is upon the earth. And God said unto Noah, This is the token of the covenant, which I have established between Me and all flesh that is upon the earth."

This Noachian covenant is an unconditional promise from God to man and every creature on the face of the earth. The sign of this covenant is the rainbow. Notice, the rainbow is not the covenant, but only a sign of the covenant. The next covenant is with Abraham in Genesis 15: 9-21:

"And He said unto him, Take Me an heifer of three years old, and a she goat of three years old, and a ram of three years old, and a turtledove, and a young pigeon. And he took unto Him all these, and divided them in the midst, and laid each piece one against another, but the birds divided he not. And when the fowls came down upon the carcases, Abram drove them away. And when the sun was going down, a deep sleep fell upon Abram; and, lo, an horror of great darkness fell upon him. And He said unto Abram, Know of a surety that thy seed shall be a stranger in a land that is not theirs, and shall serve them; and they shall afflict them four hundred years; and also that nation, whom they shall serve, will I judge: and afterward shall they come out with great substance. And thou shalt go to thy fathers in peace; thou shalt be buried in a good old age. But in the fourth generation they shall come hither

again; for the iniquity of the Amorites is not yet full. And
it came to pass, that, when the sun went down, and it was
dark, behold a smoking furnace, and a burning lamp that
passed between those pieces. In the same day the LORD
made a covenant with Abram, saying, Unto thy seed have
I given this land, from the river of Egypt unto the great
river, the river Euphrates: The Kenites, and the Kenizzites,
and the Kadmonites, and the Hittites, and the Perizzites,
and the Rephaims, and the Amorites, and the Canaanites,
and the Girgashites, and the Jebusites."

Notice the elaborate ritual God required of Abraham before
He gave him the unconditional promise of the land. The ritual
was not the covenant, nor was it a condition. It was simply a
method of signing the covenant before it was granted. Also notice
the prophecies imbedded in this passage; all of which have been
fulfilled, including the land grant. According to scholars the "river
of Egypt" is not referring to the Nile, but the Wadi el-Arish.

In the seventeenth chapter of Genesis is found another covenant
with Abraham where God agrees to be his God and the God of his
descendants. This covenant was conditional on the symbolism
of circumcision. Circumcision was not the covenant, only the
condition of the covenant.

The next covenant in Scripture is between God and Israel in the
wilderness after He has brought them out of Egypt. This covenant
is found in chapters 19-24, in the book of Exodus. The condition
for this covenant—agreement—is given in chapter 19: 1-8:

"In the third month, when the children of Israel were
gone forth out of the land of Egypt, the same day came
they into the wilderness of Sinai, for they were departed
from Rephidim, and were come to the desert of Sinai, and
had pitched in the wilderness; and there Israel camped
before the mount. And Moses went up unto God, and the
LORD called unto him out of the mountain, saying, Thus
shalt thou say to the house of Jacob, and tell the children
of Israel; ye have seen what I did unto the Egyptians,
and how I bare you on eagles' wings, and brought you

unto Myself. Now therefore, if ye will obey My voice indeed, and keep My covenant, then ye shall be a peculiar treasure unto Me above all people, for all the earth is Mine; and ye shall be unto Me a kingdom of priests, and an holy nation. These are the words which thou shalt speak unto the children of Israel. And Moses came and called for the elders of the people, and laid before their faces all these words which the LORD commanded him. And all the people answered together, and said, All that the LORD hath spoken we will do. And Moses returned the words of the people unto the LORD."

In this passage, God tells the Israelites that "if ye will obey My voice indeed, and keep My covenant," then He will be their God and they will be His people and will receive His protection and providence. What He is saying here seems plain to me. Obedience is God's condition for the agreement. In chapter twenty He formally gives them His Ten Commandment Law, which is not the covenant but the condition they must meet if they are to receive His end of the agreement. As Scripture unfolds we see that the Israelites failed to live up to their part of the covenant over and over again, but when they repented of their disobedience, and again began to obey God's Ten Commandment Law, they again began to receive His promised blessings. In the New Testament the rules are still the same. God (Christ) fulfilled prophecy and shed His blood for the sins of the world. Because of His sacrifice everyone; past, present, and future can receive His promise of eternal life with Him if we meet His condition of submission and obedience. Obeying His Ten Commandment Law is not the covenant but the condition in the Old Testament and the New Testament.

Many believe the New Testament has replaced the truth in the Old Testament. There are many truths in the Old Testament that have expired because they applied to local or time limited situations and there are Old Testament truths that are universal and timeless such as those contained in the Proverbs and Psalms. Also there are prophecies that are yet to be fulfilled and will be, just as accurately as those that have already been fulfilled.

Learning obedience through suffering

When God started us on this journey toward redemption we were forced to experience a number of things. As soon as we become conscious as babies we become aware that we must obey certain laws. The law of gravity forces itself upon us at a very early age. Striking ourselves with a heavy object teaches us a certain lesson. We learn the law of cause and effect. Suffering moves us away from wrong behavior. As children, we learn that we must live according to certain agreed upon rules in order to avoid pain and maintain peace. Children are always making up different games when they gather together and the first thing they do is establish rules by which to play those games. Playmates punish any child who will not play according to their established rules.

As children we also learn to live according to the rules established by our parents. To violate those rules results in suffering. The parents have the experience of producing a child who they love and for whom they care, suffer and sacrifice. In so doing they experience something of the joy God experienced when He created them. As their children grow into adolescents and begin to become independent and perhaps rebel and go in ways the parents think are harmful, they experience the sadness God experienced when they rebelled against Him and went their own way against His will. Over and over we experience the results of our own mistakes and as we do we suffer and learn. We also suffer from the mistakes of others such as being injured or killed in an accident caused by a drunk. And when we die I believe we evaluate our mistakes and return in another body at a time and place that will give us the opportunity to work on weaknesses in our character. The condition of our new body will reflect what we have thought said and done in the past. If we found pleasure in blinding our enemies in the past we may be born blind.

If we were that drunk who injured others we may be born in a body that is crippled. And so through the law of cause and effect we experience the consequences of our way that seems right in our own eyes but leads to destruction and death. "There is a way which seemeth right to a man, but the end thereof are the ways of death" (Pr. 14:12; 16:25).

There were times when someone would come to Edgar Cayce with a problem that was the result of something that person had done in a past life. One such case was a young boy who had a severe bed-wetting problem. His parents had been to several doctors without success. When they heard about Cayce, they wrote to him explaining the problem. In trance, he explained the problem was the result of a former life in New England during the witch trials. Women accused of witchcraft were placed in a basket on the end of a long pole and dunked in a body of water. The boy had the job, in his former lifetime, of dunking them. Cayce explained that his problem was not the fact that he dunked them but that he relished and thoroughly enjoyed his job. His attitude was the real problem. In his present lifetime he was paying for his cruel attitude by waking up soaking wet every morning. He was reaping what he had sown in a former lifetime. His parents were told to read the Bible to him every night at bedtime. They did, and the therapy worked.

Another case similar to that had to do with a man who was born blind because in a former lifetime he enjoyed blinding his enemies after a successful battle in war. This was before Christ when it was common for the victors to put out the eyes of the defeated. The problem was not so much what he did but that he enjoyed doing it. We are always the sum total of our every thought, word and deed. Sooner or later we always reap what we have sown, not out of vengeance, but so we can experience the results of our past thoughts, words and deeds, learn from them, and make corrections. We also reap the benefits from our positive thoughts, words and deeds. Our ultimate goal is perfection, which is impossible without Christ as we learn in Matthew 19:25,26: "When his disciples heard *it*, they were exceedingly amazed, saying, Who then can be saved? But Jesus beheld *them*, and said unto them, With men this is impossible; but with God all things are possible." Once we reach the point where we grasp the fact that our only salvation is to repent of our sins, submit to Jesus Christ as LORD and obey His Ten Commandment Law, and we apply that fact in our lives without ceasing, we will have fulfilled our purpose for existence and we will no longer need to reincarnate. I will go into more detail about that later.

CHAPTER SIX

REINCARNATION

Of all the many doctrines in the Bible, I believe the most important is salvation. Some facts are mentioned in passing, such as the statement that the earth is circular: "It is He that sitteth upon the circle of the earth" (Isa. 40:22). And that the earth is suspended on nothing: "He . . . hangeth the earth upon nothing" (Job 26:7). By the way, these are two of many statements proving the divine authorship of the Bible. These statements were placed in Scripture at a time when people had quite different ideas about the earth. Such ideas as the earth being supported on an elephant's back which was standing on the back of a giant turtle; or that a huge man named Atlas was supporting the earth on his back. From their perspective, the earth appeared flat, which makes sense when you think about it. When we look at the world from where we are standing it does look flat, doesn't it? It's natural to believe it is flat unless we can see it from a different perspective, like from the moon, which we can now do. So I wouldn't be too judgmental about those past flat-earth people. But when someone who claims He created everything and everyone reveals in Scripture, thousands of years before anyone ever thought of going to the moon, that the earth is round and hangs on nothing, it is hard to believe Scripture is not from God, isn't it? At any rate there are some Bible teachings that are extremely important such as salvation and there are others mentioned in passing that are not that important. I believe reincarnation falls into the second category. One trouble with the word reincarnation is that it means different things to different people.

Edgar Cayce

At this point, I believe I should take time to define reincarnation as I understand it. First I will have to admit that my definition of how reincarnation works did not come from the Bible. Some time ago, I began reading about a clairvoyant named Edgar Cayce. He was a deeply religious fundamentalist Christian who regularly taught Sunday school. As a young man he discovered he had the gift of clairvoyance and was able to help sick people by going into a special sleep or trance and then diagnosing their illnesses and recommending therapy. His formal education did not go beyond the eighth grade but in trance he used technical medical terms that even he did not understand when he woke up. Doctors had pronounced many who came to him as hopeless and yet when the therapy was applied, that Cayce recommended, they recovered. Thousands of medical records make Cayce the best-documented clairvoyant in history. Here are some true stories that demonstrate that fact:

Once Cayce was on a train and several fellow passengers invited him to a game of poker. He declined, but they insisted, so he finally agreed. After the first hand was dealt he asked everyone to wait a minute. Then he told everyone exactly what cards they were holding and the exact order of the cards in the rest of the deck. Then he asked them if they really wanted him to play poker with them. I am sure you can guess their answer. He was able to name every card in a deck from top to bottom or bottom to top after it had been thoroughly shuffled so that no one knew the sequence of the cards. This demonstrated true clairvoyance rather than mind reading.

Another time Cayce received a letter at his home in Virginia Beach, Virginia from a man in Canada. He had received medical help from Cayce a few years before and thought he might be able to help the police solve a murder, since they were at a dead end in their investigation. All they had was a body with a bullet hole in him. Cayce wrote back describing the circumstances of the murder in vivid detail, revealing the make of revolver and the serial number used in the murder and the exact location where it could be found, by a bridge in the river. He also gave the name of the victim and the name and address of the murderer. After the police found the revolver in the exact place Cayce said it was, with the serial number, they went to the address he gave them and when the murderer was confronted with the evidence he confessed. The police then put out a warrant for Cayce's arrest. They reasoned no one could possibly have that much information unless he was an accomplice. Cayce easily proved he had nothing to do with the murder.

One time Cayce told a woman to take oil of smoke as part of her therapy. She wrote back saying she couldn't find it in her city. Cayce gave her the address of a certain drug store that had it. She wrote back that the drug store did not have it. He told her to tell them to look on a certain shelf in the back room behind some bottles that he described in detail and they would find it. They found it exactly where Cayce said it was. The owner had recently bought the store and hadn't gotten around to cleaning out that old dusty shelf. Cayce had never been in that city which was over one thousand miles from his home in Virginia Beach.

After several thousand physical "readings" as they were called, some interested people started asking Cayce, while he was in his trance, questions such as where did we come from, why are we here, where do we go after death, etc. One thing he said repeatedly was that the Bible is true and accurate and if he ever said anything that contradicted Scripture we should believe Scripture rather than him. When I read that I was an agnostic and had been taught since childhood to regard the Bible as a collection of fables, superstitions, exaggerations and falsehoods. Cayce constantly advised people to accept Christ as their Lord and Savior and warned against such practices as spiritualism, medium-ship, Ouija boards, automatic writing, occultism, etc. On several occasions he warned against contacting the dead, saying they don't know any more out of their bodies than they did in them.

It has been pointed out to me that the Bible condemns psychic practices. One passage they point to is Deuteronomy 18:10-12:

"There shall not be found among you any one that maketh his son or his daughter to pass through the fire, or that useth divination, [the art or act of foretelling future events or revealing occult knowledge by means of augury or an alleged supernatural agency] or an observer of times, or an enchanter, or a witch, Or a charmer, or a consulter with familiar spirits, or a wizard, or a necromancer [the practice of supposedly communicating with the spirits of the dead in order to predict the future]. For all that do these things are an abomination unto the LORD: and because of these abominations the LORD thy God doth drive them out from before thee."

Notice clairvoyance is not mentioned, which is:

> **1.** The supposed power to see objects or events that cannot be perceived by the senses.
> **2.** Acute intuitive insight or perceptiveness.

At first I considered Cayce to be infallible in trance, since all his physical readings proved to be accurate; and I began to believe the Bible, but only according to Cayce. Later I discovered what seemed to me to be contradictions in some of his statements. One apparent glaring contradiction was his answer to the question when Jesus was born. He gave three different dates for His birth! The question was asked several years apart, three different times by three different people. This discovery ended my belief in Cayce's infallibility at that time in areas that could not be proven. Later I learned the reason for the discrepancy is he was using different ways of telling time based on the lifetime of the person for whom he was giving the reading. His physical readings were always proven to be accurate and can be checked to this day since all documentation is on record at the Association for Research and Enlightenment in Virginia Beach, Virginia.

Fortunately, by the time I began to suspect Cayce was not always accurate in his spiritual readings I had studied the Bible for several years and had concluded, independently of Cayce's assurance, that it is indeed God's inspired word. So even though at that time I was convinced Cayce was wrong about at least two of Jesus' birth dates, he was not wrong about everything; especially the fact that the Bible is God's inspired word. I also read commentaries about the Bible that proved to me that evolution is not true, that God the Creator does exist and that the Bible is His infallible word. The three best books I have found on these subjects are: *In the Beginning* by Walt Brown, *Evidence That Demands a Verdict* by Josh McDowell, and *Creation's Tiny Mystery* by Robert V. Gentry, a scientist.

Brown's book consists of three parts:

Part I: The Scientific Case for Creation, containing 131 categories of scientific evidence that support a sudden creation and oppose gradual evolution.

Part II: Fountains of the Great Deep, showing flaws in current geological explanations and that *a global flood, with vast and unique consequences, did occur.* For example, coal, oil, and methane did not form over hundreds of millions of years; they formed in months. Fossils and layered strata did not form over a billion years; they formed in months. The Grand Canyon did not form in millions of years; it formed in weeks. Major mountain ranges did not form over hundreds of millions of years; each formed in hours. These statements may appear shocking, until one has examined the evidence in Part II.

Part III: Frequently Asked Questions. Most questions concerning origins are answered in Parts I and II. Of the questions that remain, these are some of the most frequently asked in Brown's seminars and public presentations.

Not only does Brown present scientifically valid information supporting his conclusions, but he also quotes hundreds of scientists who confirm them, such as:

Scott Tremaine, David Stevenson, William R. Ward, Robin M. Canup, Fred Hoyle, Michael J. Drake, Kevin Righter, George W. Wetherill, Richard A. Kerr, Luke Dones, B. Zuckerman, Renu Malhotra, David W. Hughes, M. Mitchell Waldrop, Larry W.

Esposito, Shigeru Ida, Jack J. Lissauer, Charles Petit, P. Lamy, L. F. Miranda, Rob Rye, William R. Kuhn, Carl Sagan, Christopher Chyba, Stephen W. Hawking, Don N. Page, Huw Price, Peter Coles, Jayant V. Narlikar, Edward R. Harrison, Govert Schilling, Eric J. Lerner, Francesco Sylos Labini, Marcus Chown, Adam Riess, James Glanz, Mark Sincell, John Travis, Will Saunders, H.C. Arp, Gerard Gilmore, Geoffrey R. Burbidge, Ben Patrusky, Bernard Carr, Robert Irion, Alan H. Guth, Alexander Hellemans, Robert Matthews, M. Hattori, Lennox L. Cowie, Antoinette Songaila, Chandra Wickramasinghe, A. R. King, M. G. Watson, Charles J. Lada, Frank H. Shu, Martin Harwit, Michael Rowan-Robinson, P.J.E. Peebles, Joseph Silk, Margaret J. Geller, John P. Huchra, Larry Azar, J.E. O'Rourke, Peter Forey, J. L. B. Smith, Bryan Sykes, Edward M. Golenberg, Jeremy Cherfas, Scott R. Woodward, Virginia Morell, Hendrick N. Poinar, Rob DeSalle, Raúl J. Cano, Tomas Lindahl, George O. Poinar, Jr., Monica K. Borucki, Joshua Fischman, John Parkes, Russell H. Vreeland, Gerard Muyzer, Robert V. Gentry, Jeffrey S. Wicken, Henry R. Schoolcraft, Thomas H. Benton, Bland J. Finlay, Peter R. Sheldon, Roger Lewin, etc.

The above scientists were quoted from the following peer review science journals:

American journal of science
Astronomical journal
Astrophysics and space science
Astrophysical journal
Bioscience
Geology
Icarus
Journal of Theoretical Biology
Nature
New scientist
Physics Today
Physical review
Physical review d
Physical review letters
Science

Space science reviews
The American Journal of Science and Arts

McDowell's book is an excellent apologetic of the Bible. Beginning as a skeptic and unbeliever he accepted a challenge to disprove the Bible and as the result of his serious study of the Bible became a believer. In his book he proves the existence of God and the divine authorship of the Holy Bible using logic based on several scientific disciplines.

Gentry's book confirms the divine creation of the universe using unique scientific evidence and logic. Gentry became interested in the phenomenon of radioactive "halos" imbedded in granite—known as Precambrian granites or the Genesis rocks. Even though he had been brought up in a conservative religious environment that conflicted with the evolutionary concept, he later accepted evolution as true simply because it was taught as fact in a graduate physics course in cosmology.

The radioactive "halos" he studied in granite presented him with a serious conflict because according to the evolution model of beginnings the earth and the other planets originated by material being pulled away from the sun by a passing star several billion years ago. As the earth gradually cooled over millions of years granite became the foundation rock. Gentry was mystified by the belief that even though it took millions of years for the granite to cool to a solid state, the microscopic bits of radioactive material (^{218}Po) which caused the tiny "halos" to appear only had a half life of three minutes. He confirmed that these "halos" appear in granite worldwide and there is no evidence that they were carried in from outside by water or any other means. They were sealed in granite apparently since the granite first appeared on earth. So how did they get there? This question puzzled him for quite awhile. Then one evening a verse from the Bible popped into his head from his childhood experience in church: "By the word of the LORD were the heavens made, and all the host of them by the breath of His mouth" (Ps. 33:6). He concluded that this had to be the only answer. Those tiny "halos" had to have been placed there by God when He created everything. The earth, including the Genesis rock, was created at the same time and the "halos" represented

God's fingerprints. Most of the scientific community rejected his conclusions even though they were unable to find a better one. Also the government withdrew funding for any further research in this area. There seems to be a strong anti-God attitude in the government and the scientific community.

As the years passed and I continued my study of Scripture, my interest in Cayce's readings faded even though he had been instrumental in leading me to a serious study of the Bible. I discovered that his claim that reincarnation is a fact of life was not only *not* denied in Scripture but that the Bible actually seems to confirm it. Had I not read about Cayce I am not sure I would ever have come to the Bible and salvation through Christ. Many people think Cayce was a tool of the devil. If so, isn't it strange that I, and thousands of others, have been lead to Christ by a study of his readings? He appealed to people such as myself who would not normally be interested in the Bible.

But what are we to do with His teaching that reincarnation is a fact? Most churches are totally against such a doctrine. Is it possible they could be mistaken? After all, they have been wrong in the past, haven't they? Consider the Middle Ages when the Roman Catholic Church had a monopoly on religion in Europe. One of their unbiblical doctrines at that time was that the earth was the center of the universe and everything rotated around it. Then a man named Galileo came along with a telescope and mathematical calculations and pointed out that the earth rotates around the sun along with the other planets. The authorities ordered him to recant. He protested that he was correct and invited them to look through his telescope and examine his calculations. They refused, telling him the Bible clearly states that the earth is the center of the universe and if he did not recant he would be burned at the stake. Not wishing to die over such a question at the hands of such entrenched ignorance, he recanted publically, but not privately.

Why was the Sabbath replaced by Sunday?

Of course the Bible does not clearly state that the earth is the center of the universe. The church was wrong and Galileo was right. The information he discovered is not to be found in the Bible.

Nevertheless it is true. The Bible does not comment on everything but where it does comment it is accurate. The reason there are so many different beliefs based on the Bible is because people bring their own preconceived ideas to it and make it say things it doesn't really say. A good example of this is the belief that the Sabbath was replaced by Sunday. The Bible teaches that the Sabbath day is the seventh day of the week. Most churches keep Sunday as a holy day despite the fact that nowhere in Scripture is there any command for such a change. A little investigation reveals that Sunday keeping is a tradition handed down by the Roman Catholic Church in defiance of clear instructions in the Bible. As a matter of fact they cheerfully admit this in their official publications. They even seem to be boasting about the fact that since they changed observance from the Sabbath to Sunday, "for which there is no Scriptural authority," that this proves that the church is greater than Scripture. In the Convert's Catechism of Catholic Doctrine, 1910, page 50, whose treatise received the apostolic blessing of Pius X, January 25, 1910, we find:

> **Q.** Which is the Sabbath Day?
> **A.** Saturday is the Sabbath Day.
> **Q.** Why do we observe Sunday instead of Saturday?
> **A.** We observe Sunday instead of Saturday because the Catholic Church, in the Council of Laodicea (A.D. 336), transferred the solemnity from Saturday to Sunday.

Consider the following question and answer:

> **Q.** Have you any other way of proving that the church has power to institute festivals or precepts?
> **A.** Had she not such power, she could not have done that in which all modern religionists agree with her—she could not have substituted the observance of Sunday the first day of the week, for the observance of Saturday the seventh day, a change for which there is no Scriptural authority.—Rev. Stephen Keenan, "A Doctrinal Catechism," p. 174. New York: Edward Dunigan and Brothers, 1851.

Defining reincarnation

Just because reincarnation is not a primary doctrine in Scripture does not mean it is not true. Recently investigators have been studying the phenomenon of children remembering their past lives. Children five years and younger have talked about experiences they remembered in past lives. Interviews with these children, their parents, relatives and friends, and the people with whom they claimed to have associated in their past lives revealed that these children were not just imagining their claims. Twenty such cases are listed in the book, *Twenty Cases Suggestive of Reincarnation* by Ian Stevenson, M.D.

There are many ideas about how reincarnation works. Most of these ideas come from the Hindu and Buddhist religions, which include such beliefs as reincarnating as animals, bugs, etc. and through the concept of karma—reaping what we sow—we always receive what we deserve and therefore should not attempt to aid those in need for fear of interfering with their karma and their growth. I have noticed that when church leaders give a sermon condemning reincarnation they always use the concept of reincarnation as it is taught by these religions and they are right; the Bible does condemn reincarnation as taught by these religions. But Cayce presented a different definition that I find acceptable, reasonable and not in conflict with Scripture. Here are some basic points he made:

> ➤ We always return as humans, not as animals.

> ➤ We are spirit entities who inhabit physical bodies.

> ➤ Karma does not prohibit us from helping those in need. Rather, by helping others we create good karma, which is beneficial to all.

> ➤ All our memories, skills, personality and character are in our minds, which are spiritual, in contrast with our brains, which are physical.

➢ The brain is merely the physical instrument through which the spiritual mind expresses itself.

➢ The spiritual mind survives the death of the physical brain.

When we enter a new body shortly before or after birth we manifest through that body. It is as if we put on a coat, wear it until it wears out, then take it off and put on a new one. Peter alluded to this when he wrote; "Yea, I think it meet, as long as I am in this tabernacle [body], to stir you up by putting you in remembrance, knowing that shortly I must put off this my tabernacle, even as our Lord Jesus Christ hath shewed me" (2 Pet. 1:13,14).

Whatever we choose to think, say and do affects our future. Through the law of cause and effect we constantly reap what we have sown and what we are sowing in the present we will reap in the future.

"Be not deceived, God is not mocked, for whatsoever a man soweth, that shall he also reap. For he that soweth to his flesh shall of the flesh reap corruption, but he that soweth to the Spirit shall of the Spirit reap life everlasting" (Gal. 6:7,8).

When our bodies die we may remain in the spirit realm for years or decades or even centuries before returning to another experience on earth. On the other hand, some return within days of their death. While in the spirit we experience other areas of opportunity for learning. The time between incarnations is determined by many factors among which are opportunity and need. As we continue in one lifetime after another we have the opportunity to experience the results of our own thoughts, words and deeds. We experience wealth and poverty, justice and injustice, love and hate, kindness and cruelty. We experience the whole range of human activity. One lifetime may find us as a white landlord in charge of black slaves. The next lifetime might find us as a black slave subject to a white landlord. Every incarnation is designed by God to give us the opportunity to experience the effects of our own thoughts, words and deeds.

This is the way reincarnation works according to Edgar Cayce. It sounds reasonable to me but I know of no proof that he is right, nor does the Bible confirm or deny his explanation. How reincarnation works is not explained in the Bible but I believe the Bible does teach that it is a fact of life and I choose to believe that Cayce is probably accurate as to how it operates simply because it makes sense to me and does not conflict with Scripture.

Natural body/spiritual body

Here is a Bible passage that could be interpreted to mean that my understanding of origins is incorrect:

> "There is a natural body, and there is a spiritual body. And so it is written, The first man Adam was made a living soul; the last Adam *was made* a quickening spirit. Howbeit that *was* not first which is spiritual, but that which is natural; and afterward that which is spiritual. The first man *is* of the earth, earthy: the second man *is* the Lord from heaven. As *is* the earthy, such *are* they also that are earthy: and as *is* the heavenly, such *are* they also that are heavenly. And as we have borne the image of the earthy, we shall also bear the image of the heavenly" (1 Cor. 15:44-49).

On the surface it would seem that this contradicts my understanding of origins. If it is saying the physical body was created before the spiritual, then it does indeed contradict my understanding that we were first created spirit beings and then later given physical bodies through which to express ourselves in a physical, three dimensional plane. But is that what is really meant here? I don't think so, and neither do most scholars.

The contrast is not between the natural (material) body and the spiritual (immaterial) body but rather a physical body that is subject to death and a spiritual body that is not. Paul is not saying the physical body was created first but is using the analogy of the first Adam who had a physical body and was therefore mortal, and the second Adam, Christ, who gave us the opportunity to receive spiritual, immortal bodies by His sacrifice for us. Our resurrected bodies will be like His glorified physical, resurrected body, which was free from all physical corruption and limitations. The sinful nature came first and resulted in our being mortal. Christ came to earth and shed His blood in our place, making it possible for us to attain His righteous nature and become immortal.

The consequences of Christ's delay

There is a popular belief taught today by most churches that the reason Christ is taking so long to return and wind things up is because He is giving the unsaved more time to discover the error of their ways, repent, and receive salvation. On the surface this sounds reasonable but if we look a little closer I think we can detect a flaw in this reasoning. According to their theology every birth is a newly created human. If we apply that belief we come to a disturbing conclusion. Since the cross billions of people have been born, lived and died, and of that multitude only a very small fraction have been saved. This is still true today, isn't it? So every day that Christ delays His return, millions of people are born who will never be saved and will go to hell for eternity if it is true that every birth is a newly created soul. So even though there are a few out of that number who will find Christ and salvation, the vast majority will not. Isn't it a shame that His delay is resulting in so many additional souls going to eternal torment?

On the other hand, if reincarnation is a fact then instead of new souls being created at the time of every birth, every soul that now exists was created in the beginning. We are all the same age. Now Christ's delay makes sense. The longer He waits, the more souls will be converted and the fewer will be lost since the total number of souls remains the same but the ratio between the saved and the lost constantly changes in favor of salvation.

Part of God's plan of salvation

I believe God made reincarnation part of His plan of salvation so that we could have the time necessary to try out all our ideas that we think will bring us what we want without His help. That's what our rebellion was all about. We think we can create our own paradise in our own wisdom and strength and God has given us this opportunity to try out our ideas and prove to ourselves whether or not they will work. He knows we will fail but He has given us time and opportunity to discover this for ourselves as in the parable of the Prodigal Son (Lk. 15:11-32). We have also been given the time to realize our error and return to Him:

> "And even as they did not like to retain God in their knowledge, God gave them over to a reprobate [depraved] mind, to do those things which are not convenient [proper, suitable or fitting]; being filled with all unrighteousness, fornication, wickedness, covetousness, maliciousness; full of envy, murder, debate, deceit, malignity; whisperers, backbiters, haters of God, despiteful, proud, boasters, inventors of evil things, disobedient to parents, without understanding, covenantbreakers, without natural affection, implacable, unmerciful. Who knowing the judgment of God, that they which commit such things are worthy of death, not only do the same, but have pleasure in them that do them" (Rom. 1:28-32).

Looks like today's newspaper, doesn't it? This is God's evaluation of the reality of unredeemed human nature. Just before the Noachian Flood we are told: "And GOD saw that the wickedness of man was great in the earth, and that every imagination of the thoughts of his heart was only evil continually" (Gen. 6:5). After the flood, He said, ". . . the imagination of man's heart is evil from his youth..." (Gen. 8:21). The flood didn't improve human nature, did it?

Of course God already knows the end from the beginning, but we are not willing to listen to Him, are we? We think our way is best and we don't need Him. We continue to follow the spirit of rebellion—Satan. And so down through the centuries we have written the history of this experiment. And what a bloody history it has been right up the present time when wickedness is increasing worldwide between individuals and nations as predicted in Scripture:

> "This know also, that in the last days perilous times shall come. For men shall be lovers of their own selves, covetous, boasters, proud, blasphemers, disobedient to parents, unthankful, unholy, without natural affection, trucebreakers, false accusers, incontinent [without self control], fierce, despisers of those that are good, traitors, heady, highminded, lovers of pleasures more than lovers of God; having a form of godliness, but denying the power thereof. From such turn away" (2 Tim. 3:1-5).

By the way, notice in this passage that all of these destructive activities are said to be caused by men (mankind), not Satan. When we live outside of God's will these are the results and they are Satanic, which confirms my belief that Satan is the symbolic personification of ungodly, disobedient, rebellious human nature. When I look at what is going on in the world it does seem that these traits are predominant. People seem to be more interested in seeking pleasure than God and His righteousness. "For many walk, of whom I have told you often, and now tell you even weeping, that they are the enemies of the cross of Christ, whose end is destruction, whose God is their belly, and whose glory is in their shame, who mind earthly things" (Phlp. 3:18,19). They worship the god of pleasure instead of the one and only true, living creator God. One example is abortion, which is the result of placing pleasure above everything including human life! Is there any greater example of wickedness than this? I don't think it is an exaggeration to say that today the womb has become a tomb and is the most dangerous place on earth!

I think if anyone reads the history of human experience and the daily newspaper he will come to the conclusion that we haven't done too well toward creating our own paradise without God's help, have we? As a matter of fact, all the evidence points in the opposite direction, doesn't it? And yet despite this overwhelming evidence we continue to turn our backs on God and try our own ideas. We are incredibly hardheaded! But even though God has given us over to a reprobate (depraved) mind (Rom. 1:28), that does not mean He has abandoned us forever. Since the wages of sin is death, God probably would have executed us if He had given up on us. The fact that we are still alive means He is still allowing us to run our course in the hope that we will finally realize our lost condition, repent and return to Him. I believe this is the primary purpose of life. "Let us hear the conclusion of the whole matter: Fear God, and keep His Commandments, for this is the whole duty of man" (Ecc. 12:13).

Are we immortal?

Reincarnation does not mean we are immortal as some imagine. God says:

> ➢ ". . . the soul that sinneth, it shall die" (Ezek. 18:4).

> ➢ "For the wages of sin is death" (Rom. 6:23).

> ➢ "And fear not them which kill the body, but are not able to kill the soul, but rather fear Him which is able to destroy both soul and body in hell" (Mt. 10:28).

God says we are mortal. In fact, He declares that only He is immortal, ". . . our Lord Jesus Christ . . . who only has immortality" (1 Tim. 6:14,16). The fact that we survive the death of our body does not mean we are immortal, any more than surviving the "death" of our coat means we are immortal. We survive our bodies from one experience to another but until we receive immortality from God we remain mortal in each lifetime and between lifetimes—in the flesh or out of the flesh. If we stubbornly remain on the broad, smooth road that leads to the lake of fire, our final destination is eternal death.

Many believe that we are now immortal and can never die spiritually, so when our bodies die we go to heaven or hell. Or if reincarnation is true we just keep on trying until we get it right, and eventually everyone goes to heaven. The belief in universal salvation is interesting but I believe it contradicts Scripture. It is true that God desires all to be saved, but it is also true that unless they repent of their sins, submit to Jesus Christ as LORD and obey His Ten Commandment Law He will:

> ". . . rise up as *in* mount Perazim, he shall be wroth as *in* the valley of Gibeon, that he may do his work, his strange work; and bring to pass his act, his strange act. Now therefore be ye not mockers, lest your bands be made strong: for I have heard from the Lord GOD of hosts a consumption [destruction], even determined upon the whole earth" (Isa. 28:21,22).

God is life, not death, but He is also holy and just and after all else fails He will reluctantly and sadly destroy the disobedient. Jesus said:

> ➤ ". . . except ye repent, ye shall all likewise perish" (Lk. 13: 3,5).

> ➤ "For God so loved the world, that he gave his only begotten Son, that whosoever believeth in him should not perish, but have everlasting life" (John 3:16).

Here we have a contrast between perish and everlasting life. The definition of everlasting life is obvious—eternal life. The definition of perish must therefore be the opposite of everlasting life—eternal death. In 2 Peter 3:9 we learn, "The Lord is not slack concerning his promise, as some men count slackness; but is longsuffering to us-ward, not willing that any should perish, but that all should come to repentance." If we are to avoid eternal death, we must repent. The notion that we now have eternal life is not true. God reveals:

> "But after thy hardness and impenitent heart treasurest up unto thyself wrath against the day of wrath and revelation of the righteous judgment of God; Who will render to every man according to his deeds: To them

who by patient continuance in well doing seek for glory
and honour and immortality, eternal life" (Rom. 2:5-7).

Why would we have to seek immortality if we already have it?
Here's another one: "For this corruptible must put on incorruption,
and this mortal *must* put on immortality" (1 Cor. 15:53). If we
already have immortality we won't have to put it on, will we? It
seems obvious to me that we are now mortal, both physically and
spiritually.

Our lives are longer than it seems from our limited perspective,
having been created before Genesis 1:2 when we were all created
at the same time. Reincarnation is as temporary as God's plan of
salvation. After the millennium God will end His plan of salvation.
Then the unrighteous and wicked will be destroyed forever in the
lake of fire. When Christ returns the second time to gather His
saints at the beginning of His thousand year reign they ". . . shall
not all sleep, but [they] shall all be changed, in a moment, in the
twinkling of an eye, at the last trump. For the trumpet shall sound,
and the dead shall be raised incorruptible, and [they] shall be
changed. For this corruptible must put on incorruption, and this
mortal must put on immortality" (1 Cor. 15:51-53).

Eternal life is attained through repentance in the name of Jesus
Christ. Until we repent of our sins, submit to Jesus Christ as our
LORD and obey His Ten Commandment Law, He cannot be our
savior. We must repent of our sins (lawbreaking—1 John 3:4) and
desire to obey God. He will not have anyone in His Kingdom who
will not submit to His will and obey Him:

> ➤ "Not every one that saith unto Me, Lord, Lord,
> shall enter into the Kingdom of Heaven, but he that
> doeth the will of My Father which is in heaven" (Mt.
> 7:21).

> ➤ ". . . if thou wilt enter into life, keep the Commandments"
> (Mt. 19:17).

Only when we repent in the name of Jesus Christ for the
forgiveness of our sins (Acts 2:38) and submit to His Lordship

will God forgive us all our sins and give us eternal life, not as a reward but because Christ paid the penalty for our sins with His own blood. When God's plan of salvation has run its course there will be a judgment. In the meantime God, in His love, has given us a way to regain our lost condition. But first, we must suffer in the pigpen of sin until we finally are sick of it and long to return to our heavenly Father. "The Lord is not slack concerning His promise, as some men count slackness; but is longsuffering to us-ward, not willing that any should perish, but that all should come to repentance (2 Pet. 3:9).

CHAPTER SEVEN

REINCARNATION IN THE BIBLE?

There are several places in Scripture that seem to hint at the reality of reincarnation:

Seeking God after death

> "When He slew them, then they sought Him, and they returned and enquired early after God" (Ps. 78:34).

Did they seek Him *after* He slew them? It looks like it, doesn't it?

Jeremiah before conception

> "Then the word of the LORD came unto me, saying: Before I formed thee in the belly I knew thee, and before thou camest forth out of the womb I sanctified thee, and I ordained thee a prophet unto the nations" (Jer. 1:4,5).

God is telling Jeremiah that He knew him before he was even conceived in the womb and ordained him to be a prophet before his birth. How did God know Jeremiah was qualified to be a prophet before he was conceived in the womb, unless he existed before he was conceived? And how did Jeremiah qualify to be a prophet of God before he was born unless he lived in obedience and submission to God at least one lifetime before his birth as

Jeremiah? After all, think what it must take for someone to qualify as a prophet of God. Surely a person has to know God, understand His will and then choose to submit and obey. This takes time and maturity. It seems to me that Jeremiah had to have lived several lifetimes before his birth as Jeremiah.

Most people object that this simply means that God knew Jeremiah in the same sense that He knows everything and everyone past, present and future. But that doesn't explain to my satisfaction the fact that God not only said He knew Jeremiah before he was conceived, but that He ordained him as a prophet before he was born. This objection also implies that we don't exercise free will in choosing our way but that God has our future mapped out in advance. This would mean we are what we are because we have been pre-programmed this way before we were conceived. If this were true, then salvation would not be necessary since some of us are predestined for heaven, and some for hell, and nothing we think, say, or do will have any effect on our destiny. I know of no such doctrine in Scripture although there are some who express such a belief! Also, the word "knew" here means more than just know about. The deeper meaning of the word is to have a close intimate relationship. In Scripture, this is usually the way the word "know" or "knew" is used.

Jesus said John was Elijah

One of the most direct statements concerning reincarnation is found in Matthew where Jesus tells His disciples:

> ➤ "For all the prophets and the law prophesied until John. And if ye will receive it, this is Elias [Elijah], which was for to come. He that hath ears to hear, let him hear" (Mt. 11:13,14).

> ➤ "And his disciples asked him, saying, Why then say the scribes that Elias must first come? And Jesus answered and said unto them, Elias truly shall first come, and restore all things. But I say unto you, that Elias is come already, and they knew him not, but

have done unto him whatsoever they listed [wished].
Likewise shall also the Son of man suffer of them.
Then the disciples understood that he spake unto
them of John the Baptist" (Mt. 17:10-13).

We need to notice several things about these verses. The
prophecy that the disciples were referring to is found in the last two
verses in the Old Testament; Malachi 4:5,6: "Behold, I will send
you Elijah the prophet before the coming of the great and dreadful
day of the LORD, and he shall turn the heart of the fathers to the
children, and the heart of the children to their fathers, lest I come
and smite the earth with a curse." Most people explain those words
of Jesus by quoting Luke 1:17 where an angel is telling Zacharias
that he will have a son named John; "And he shall go before Him
in the spirit and power of Elias..." So they claim that Jesus meant
that John had come in the "spirit and power" of Elijah, not that
he *was* Elijah. The problem I have with that explanation is that in
Malachi 4:5 God said He would send Elijah, not someone else in
the spirit and power of Elijah. Also, Jesus said John *was* Elijah, not
that John had come in Elijah's spirit and power. As to the angel's
statement, who would be better qualified to come in the spirit and
power of Elijah than Elijah himself? Also there may be a special
significance to the word "spirit" in that statement. Perhaps we are
being told that Elijah's spirit occupied John's body, which is, after
all, what reincarnation is, isn't it?

Another objection I usually hear is that John himself denied
that he was Elijah when specifically asked (John 1:21). John may
not have known he was Elijah. Or, if he knew, he couldn't admit
it then or his ministry would have been prematurely cut short
because he hadn't yet baptized Jesus. If he had admitted he was
Elijah, the authorities probably would have arrested him on the
spot. Does this mean he lied? No, he could have denied being
Elijah and still told the truth. What they asked him was "*are* you
Elijah?" not "*were* you Elijah?" His name was Elijah in the past,
during his lifetime as Elijah, but now his name was John. So if he
knew he had been Elijah, he may have just truthfully answered
them literally in order to escape premature arrest. The fact remains
that on two separate occasions, Jesus said John *was* Elijah.

I also find it interesting that when Jesus gave this answer to His disciples He qualified His statements with "if you will receive it," and "he who has ears to hear, let him hear." These statements indicate to me that even though reincarnation is true it isn't the most important message in Scripture and therefore it isn't crucial that we believe it. It simply is a fact. Salvation is the most important message in Scripture, and a belief in reincarnation is not necessary for salvation although an understanding of reincarnation certainly answers a lot of questions that otherwise remain mysteries. Today Jesus might have said, "if the shoe fits wear it."

The rebirth of the scribes and Pharisees

During Jesus' condemnation of the hypocritical scribes and Pharisees He made this statement:

> "That upon you may come all the righteous blood
> shed upon the earth, from the blood of righteous Abel
> unto the blood of Zacharias son of Barachias, whom ye
> slew between the temple and the altar" (Mt. 23:35).

Jesus said those scribes and Pharisees to whom He was speaking had taken part in slaying Barachias between the temple and the altar, which occurred hundreds of years before they were born. Reincarnation explains how this was possible.

When do babies sin?

In Romans 3:23 we learn, "For all have sinned, and come short of the glory of God." Since "sin is the transgression of the law" (1 John 3:4) then all have transgressed the law. Since the law is the Ten Commandments, then all have transgressed the Ten Commandment Law. The word "all" is pretty inclusive, isn't it? Wouldn't that include newborn babies? But how could they have transgressed the law? Which commandment did they transgress? Obviously none in this lifetime. So they must have transgressed the Ten Commandment Law in a former lifetime.

Chosen before creation

In Ephesians 1:4 we learn that "He hath chosen us in him before the foundation of the world." It sounds like we could have existed before the foundation of the world, doesn't it?

The rapture

In 1 Thessalonians 4:15,17, Paul wrote:

> "For this we say unto you by the word of the Lord, that we which are alive and remain unto the coming of the Lord shall not prevent [precede] them which are asleep. Then we which are alive and remain shall be caught up together with them in the clouds, to meet the Lord in the air, and so shall we ever be with the Lord."

Here we find Paul writing "by the word of the Lord" that he and those to whom he is writing will be alive on earth in the flesh at the second coming of the Lord. He describes two kinds of people: the dead in Christ and those who are alive in Christ. "By the word of the Lord" he wrote that he and those to whom he was writing would be among those who would be alive in the flesh on the earth at Christ's second coming. Paul and the Thessalonians all died about two thousand years ago so if Paul was telling the truth "by the word of the Lord" then the only way I know for them to be alive in the flesh on the earth at Christ's second coming is if they reincarnate.

The objection I hear most often about this is that Paul mistakenly believed Christ would return in his lifetime. By saying that they are also saying the Lord was mistaken because Paul was simply taking His word for it. Also if we go along with this line of reasoning and admit that Paul made a false statement here, then not only was he mistaken about hearing it from the Lord, assuming the Lord does not make false statements, but then we have to wonder how many other false statements Paul made, and perhaps Paul was also deluded about being inspired by the Holy Spirit. It makes more sense to me to simply believe that the Lord and Paul were correct and reincarnation is a fact.

Another explanation I have heard is that Paul is simply describing the fact that he and his readers will be resurrected at Christ's second coming at which time they will be in the flesh of their newly resurrected bodies. But Paul is not saying that at all. Notice, he says the dead in Christ will be raised first: "Then we which are alive and remain shall be caught up together with them…" (1 Thes. 4:17). Paul is saying he and his readers will be in that second group of people who will be alive in the flesh at the second coming of Christ.

The man born blind

One day Jesus and His disciples found a man who was born blind:

> "And his disciples asked him, saying, Master, who
> did sin, this man, or his parents, that he was born blind?"
> (John 9:2).

I think it is important here that we notice what Jesus did not say as well as what He did say in His reply. First, what did Jesus fail to say? His disciple had just asked Him a question revealing that they believed a man could be born blind as the result of his own sins. They didn't ask Him *if* the man could be born blind as the result of his own sins. Their question indicated that they believed such a thing was commonplace and going on all the time. Their question revealed a belief in reincarnation. Perhaps they had accepted Jesus' explanation of John the Baptist being the reincarnation of Elijah as He had explained to them earlier. At any rate they were telling Jesus that they believed in reincarnation. After all, how else could this man have been born blind as the result of his own sins unless he had committed those sins in a previous lifetime?

These disciples were Jesus' students. He was teaching them the truth, which He was later going to send them into the world to teach. If reincarnation were not true, doesn't it seem strange that He didn't immediately correct His students? He corrected them on many other occasions. He even corrected His enemies when they made false statements. Why didn't He correct His disciples when they revealed they believed in reincarnation? I believe the answer is obvious: Reincarnation is a fact!

At this point I am usually reminded what Jesus did say in response to His disciples' question:

> "Neither hath this man sinned, nor his parents, but that the works of God should be made manifest in him" (John 9:3).

I am assured that Jesus here is telling His disciples that reincarnation is out of the question. Since He said this man was not born blind as the result of his or his parent's sins, He is telling them there is no such thing as reincarnation. On the surface we might be able to draw such a conclusion, especially if our preconceptions do not include a belief in reincarnation.

Notice that Jesus said "*this man*" is not blind as the result of his own or his parents' sins, but "that the works of God should be made manifest in him." Jesus said He was talking about "*this man*," this one special individual man who was born blind for one purpose only; so Jesus could heal him and therefore manifest the works of God in him. Can we honestly conclude that Jesus was telling His disciples and us that every man who is born blind is not born blind as the result of his own or his parents sins, but "that the works of God should be made manifest in him?" How many people have been born blind because their mothers or fathers have been sexually promiscuous and caught a venereal disease? A little research will reveal quite a few. The fact is that many people are indeed born blind as the result of the sins of their parents. If Jesus was talking about all men who have been born blind, then He was simply making a false statement.

We cannot as easily demonstrate that men are born blind as the result of their own sins but the fact remains that Jesus did not correct His disciples when they revealed a belief in reincarnation, therefore I believe we can safely conclude that reincarnation is a fact and men usually are born blind as the result of their own sins committed in a previous lifetime. Actually it would probably be more accurate to say they are born blind as the result of *both* their sins *and* their parent's sins. According to Cayce, when we seek to incarnate, we look for the circumstances that will give us the best opportunity to work on those areas in our life that will give us the experience we need to learn what we need to learn. We reap what we sow (Gal. 6:7) in order to work on those areas in our character that need improvement. Reincarnation explains why people are born with liabilities or assets that do not seem to relate to any condition of their physical birth or upbringing in this present lifetime. I believe every incarnation is designed by God to give our parents, everyone we contact and us an opportunity to find eternal life in Him.

There are a number of other places in Scripture that seem to refer to reincarnation in passing but I have mentioned the ones that I believe are the most important. I have noticed that since I have come to believe in reincarnation I see it popping up more often in Scripture. It is a little like those pictures that have things hidden in them. I usually have a hard time finding those hidden images but once I see them I have a hard time not seeing them. If I had not been told ahead of time that the picture contained those hidden images I may never have noticed them. What we are taught ahead of time is important in determining what we will see in the scriptures. Reading Scripture with preconceptions often leads us astray in our conclusions. We must carefully compare our preconceptions with Scripture. If we see a contradiction between Scripture and belief then we must change our belief to conform to Scripture in the same way that we must change our behavior to conform to God's will—His Ten Commandment Law. For unredeemed human nature this is impossible, but:

> "The things which are impossible with men are possible with God" (Lk. 18:27).

That is why we need the indwelling of the Holy Spirit to help us to understand and apply truth. In Acts 2:38 we are told how to receive the gift of the Holy Spirit: "Then Peter said unto them, Repent, and be baptized every one of you in the name of Jesus Christ for the remission of sins, and ye shall receive the gift of the

Holy Ghost." We need to remember God's definition of a Christian: "Now if any man have not the Spirit of Christ, he is none of His" (Rom. 8:9). In context we find that the Spirit of Christ in this verse is the Holy Spirit. If we do not belong to Christ we are not Christians, are we?

It is appointed unto men once to die

Another objection against reincarnation I want to deal with is one I almost always hear whenever the word "reincarnation" is mentioned. I can usually count on this knee-jerk response: ". . . it is appointed unto men once to die, but after this the judgment." This is quoted from Hebrews 9:27 and most people who do not want to believe in reincarnation believe this one part of a verse proves reincarnation does not exist. If this were the only verse in the Bible I would be inclined to agree, but when compared to the other verses I have mentioned, either this verse contradicts those verses, which means there are false statements in Scripture, or we do not correctly understand the intended meaning of either this verse or the others.

Admittedly I began to seriously believe in the existence of reincarnation because of Edgar Cayce and other sources outside the Bible. However, when I read Scripture I do find it seems to confirm those sources. Scripture does not go into minute detail on every possible subject but whatever is mentioned, even in passing, is always totally accurate. I have been accused of reading reincarnation into Scripture. I don't think so. What I have done is look at the facts, compared them with Scripture, and found that Scripture confirms those facts. Obviously those who do not wish to believe in reincarnation do believe that Hebrews 9:27 disproves reincarnation or they would not always quote it to "prove" reincarnation is false. Perhaps they are guilty of reading reincarnation out of Scripture!

Taking Hebrews 9:27 in context, I find the author is not referring to reincarnation at all. As a matter of fact, this statement is not even accurate if it is taken the way the anti-reincarnationists interpret it. They seem to believe that it is saying people die one time and then are judged and either go to heaven or hell. I thought

Scripture teaches the judgment takes place after the resurrection and after the millennium, both of which are still to occur in the future. Also if everyone is appointed to die once, then what about all the people in Scripture who died and were miraculously brought back to life? Not only was there no judgment for them, but also, assuming they died again at a later time, they died twice, didn't they? Just what is the author of Hebrews saying? Let's put the verse in context. Starting with verse 24 we read:

> "For Christ is not entered into the holy places made with hands, which are the figures of the true, but into heaven itself, now to appear in the presence of God for us. Nor yet that He should offer Himself often, as the high priest entereth into the holy place every year with blood of others, for then must He often have suffered since the foundation of the world. But now once in the end of the world hath He appeared to put away sin by the sacrifice of Himself. And as it is appointed unto men once to die, but after this the judgment, so Christ was once offered to bear the sins of many. And unto them that look for Him shall He appear the second time without sin unto salvation" (Heb. 9:24-28).

Notice that the word "once" appears three times in this passage. First we learn that Jesus appeared once to "put away sin by the sacrifice of Himself" as opposed to the fact that the high priest had to enter the holy place every year with the blood of others for atonement. Jesus shed His own blood for the sins of the world. Once appears a second time in the famous "it is appointed unto men once to die, but after this the judgment." And finally, "Christ was once offered to bear the sins of many." The second time He appears will be "without sin unto salvation."

It seems to me that the meaning in this passage is that Jesus died one time in our place for our sins. Because of our sins we once had an appointment with death and judgment but Jesus kept our appointment for us, in our place, so that if we will repent of our sins, submit to Him as LORD and obey His Ten Commandment Law we will no longer have to keep that appointment. Isaiah 28:18

seems to touch on this subject: "And your covenant with death shall be disannulled, and your agreement with hell shall not stand."

Some will argue that even though the subject of this passage is not reincarnation it certainly is a condemnation of it. I disagree. If the subject is what I think it is then reincarnation is not only not the subject, it isn't even remotely alluded to, nor does it suggest in any way that reincarnation is not a fact. As I have pointed out above, there are many scriptures that do allude to reincarnation and verify its existence.

Matthew 24

In the Olivet Prophecy, Matthew 24, we learn:

> "And Jesus went out, and departed from the temple: and his disciples came to him for to shew him the buildings of the temple. And Jesus said unto them, See ye not all these things? verily I say unto you, There shall not be left here one stone upon another, that shall not be thrown down. And as he sat upon the mount of Olives, the disciples came unto him privately, saying, Tell us, when shall these things be? and what shall be the sign of thy coming, and of the end of the world? And Jesus answered and said unto them, Take heed that no man deceive you..." (vss. 1-4).

He then proceeds to answer their questions in the next 44 verses. What I find interesting is He uses the personal pronoun "you" or an equivalent throughout. For example:

- ➤ 6 And ye shall hear of wars and rumours of wars: see that ye be not troubled.
- ➤ 9 Then shall they deliver you up to be afflicted, and shall kill you: and ye shall be hated of all nations for my name's sake.
- ➤ 15 When ye therefore shall see the abomination of desolation, spoken of by Daniel the prophet, stand in the holy place.

> ➢ 20 But pray ye that your flight be not in the winter, neither on the sabbath day.
> ➢ 23 Then if any man shall say unto you, Lo, here is Christ, or there; believe it not.
> ➢ 25 Behold, I have told you before.
> ➢ 26 Wherefore if they shall say unto you, Behold, he is in the desert; go not forth: behold, he is in the secret chambers; believe it not.
> ➢ 32 Now learn a parable of the fig tree; When his branch is yet tender, and putteth forth leaves, ye know that summer is nigh.
> ➢ 33 So likewise ye, when ye shall see all these things, know that it is near, even at the doors.
> ➢ 42 Watch therefore: for ye know not what hour your Lord doth come.
> ➢ 44 Therefore be ye also ready: for in such an hour as ye think not the Son of man cometh.

Those verses are talking about the future after the disciples have died and yet Jesus is referring to them as "you." The only way they could be there in the future is if they reincarnated.

Pierced

"Behold, he cometh with clouds; and every eye shall see him, and they also which pierced him: and all kindreds of the earth shall wail because of him" (Rev. 1:7).

Since those who pierced Jesus died centuries before His second coming, how else would they be present in the flesh unless they reincarnated?

Why don't we remember our past lives?

Usually people wonder why we don't remember our past lives if reincarnation is true. Earlier I mentioned the book *Twenty Cases Suggestive of Reincarnation* where the author tells of research he and his co-workers conducted interviewing people who, as children, remembered their past lives. People were also interviewed who had been associated with them in their past lives as well as their present lives. Events, details and records were checked to confirm that the people they claimed to be really existed.

One case from the book starting on page 52, was about a girl in India named Sukla, who was born in March, 1954. I quote: "When she was about a year and a half old and barely able to walk, she was often observed cradling a block of wood or a pillow and addressing it as 'Minu.' When asked who 'Minu' was, she said 'My daughter.'" In the next few years she revealed more information about her previous life including her former husband, his younger brothers, Khetu and Karuna, and expressed a strong desire to go to the village of Bhatpara where she had lived, which is about eleven miles from Kampa where she presently lived.

In the summer of 1959, when she was about five, Sukla was taken to Bhatpara where she led the way to the house of her former father-in-law Sri Amritalal Chakravarty. There she correctly named a number of people and objects.

Her meeting with her former husband and daughter was emotionally disturbing for all and continued to be. I quote: "The meeting of Sukla and her supposed former husband Sri Haridhan Chakravarty, and her former daughter Minu, aroused great emotion in Sukla and further longings to be with them again. Unlike some other children of these cases...she never expressed a wish to rejoin the other family permanently. But she did long for visits from Sri Haridhan Chakravarty and pined for him when he did not come."

Hugh Lynn Cayce, Edgar Cayce's son, told me a similar story about a five year old girl in India who started talking about her past life experiences in a town about one hundred miles from where she lived. She claimed she had been a mother and a wife. At first her parents dismissed her claims as the imagination of a child. But as she continued to talk about her past life it became obvious she was too young to have knowledge of some of the things she related such as details concerning her pregnancy and child bearing. The family doctor was consulted, and after listening to her, he suggested they should travel with the girl to the town in which she claimed to have lived and died.

Neither the girl nor her parents had ever been to the town but as the train neared the outskirts the girl grew more and more excited, pointing out familiar landmarks and even predicting buildings and other landmarks they were about to see. When they arrived at the house she claimed to have lived in, her former husband and children were not living there. Also she said she had buried a jewelry box under the big tree in the front yard but when she dug in the spot the box was not there.

The people who lived in the house said the former owner had sold it and moved to the other side of town after his wife died six years earlier. When they arrived at the new house the girl became very excited as the owner and his children came out to meet them. She ran up to the man, calling him by his correct name, and embraced him. Then she did the same with his children. She also mentioned personal things only the family knew about. It was an awkward moment for everyone, and also emotionally painful. The former husband said he had found the jewelry box under the tree at the old address before they moved and not only was the box exactly where the girl said it was but the contents were exactly as she had described.

The problem with this girl and Sukla remembering their past lives was it only served to cause emotional pain and suffering for them and their former families. It also tended to interfere with their ability to live normally in their present lives. This consequence was common to all the children who were investigated. I don't know why God allowed these people to remember their past lives but I do know His will is always in our best interest even though it may not always seem so to us.

So why don't we usually remember our past lives? I believe it is because these memories would interfere with our present lives. Imagine knowing that your brother was the person who raped and strangled you in a past life, for example. Just because we don't remember our past lives doesn't mean we didn't exist. How many people remember everything in this life? We spend nine months in our mother's womb but we don't remember that. Neither do we remember most of our childhood, but we existed during that time, didn't we? Most of us would be hard pressed to remember every detail of yesterday, wouldn't we?

What about increasing population?

Another objection I hear quite often is that if reincarnation is true, how do I account for the fact that the population of the world keeps increasing? My answer is to compare life with a stage play where there may be a cast of 100 but only a few appear on the stage at any one time. The rest remain off stage until their turn. The only time the whole cast appears on stage at the same time is in the grand finale. Today there are more people on earth than at any time in recorded history. Could we be approaching *our* grand finale?

Quite often we tend to believe things are true or false simply because we were taught that way from childhood and everyone else believes that way. When I was a kid, I wondered why everyone went to church on Sunday when the Bible says Saturday is the Sabbath day. I didn't even question it for years, because I assumed everyone was doing it right since everyone was doing it. Later I accepted the teaching that the Sabbath was changed to Sunday to celebrate Christ's resurrection. It was only after I began a serious study of the Bible that I discovered that there is no scriptural authority for such a change. Men, not God, made the change.

Some church groups not only transgress the Sabbath commandment, they claim the Ten Commandments have been totally done away and it is actually a sin to obey any of them despite the fact that God says, "Sin is the transgression of the law" (1 John 3:4). I believe our primary problem is lawlessness. That is why we are confined to the earth, and why, despite our intelligence, cleverness and inventiveness, we have never been able to achieve lasting peace and prosperity. Universal Sunday keeping is one of the most visible examples of the tendency of human nature to believe what it wants to believe despite what Scripture and the facts teach. The same tendency of human nature, I believe, explains why so many refuse to believe that Scripture and the facts teach reincarnation to be true. We usually see what we want to see, don't we?

CHAPTER EIGHT

OVERVIEW AND BEYOND

At this point I would like to review what I have covered and then go on to the end of man's experience, as I understand it. Remember, what I say is what I believe and could be in error, but of course I will continue to believe I am correct until I am convinced by other evidence that I am wrong. After all, I haven't always believed as I now do. My belief has changed over the years and I hope you will agree that I have good reason to believe as I now do, but I also realize I could be wrong and I welcome any proof or evidence that will persuade me that I am because I do want to know the truth. In the meantime I believe that what I believe is true. I think it is a mistake to assume that what we believe cannot be wrong. Most religions seem to have this attitude and since their minds are closed, and if they are in fact wrong, then they cannot accept the truth, can they? A good example of this is the religious leaders of Christ's day.

Our decline from harmony with God

I believe that in the beginning God created everything and everyone. At first we were created as spirit beings in the image of God including mind, spirit and free will. As free will spirit entities we were to experience God's creation and love and grow in grace and experience, finally returning to Him as true companions. About a third of us began to believe our way was better than

God's way and we began following the spirit of rebellion, which is personified by the name Satan.

God loves sinners

Since we were going contrary to God's will we were committing sin, which is defined by Him as transgressing His Ten Commandment Law (1 John 3:4). He was not surprised by our sin since He knew that was possible when He gave us free will. So from the very beginning He had His plan of salvation ready. Since His law demands death as the consequence of sin (Rom. 6:23) there was no way He could change that consequence without destroying all of creation since His law is an integral part of creation. Either we had to die for our own sins or someone had to die in our place. Since He was not willing that any should die, but that all should come to repentance (2 Pet. 3:9), He determined that He would die in our place since He is the only one who qualified. This demonstrates just how much He loves us and wants us to live with Him in eternity.

When we rebelled against God He could have destroyed us in His righteousness since the law demands the death penalty. But He also loved us and did not want to lose any of us. Also, the other two-thirds of the angels who had not sinned would never know for sure that our contrary way was not better than God's way. They would take it on faith but there would always have been that unanswered question. After all, God does tell us to "Prove all things. Hold fast that which is good" (1 Thes. 5:21).

Confined to earth

The first thing God had to do was stop us from roaming freely all over His creation, contaminating it with our rebellion. So He gathered us all up and confined us to the earth where we had such a huge temper tantrum, misusing our angelic powers, that we literally destroyed the prehistoric earth that existed at that time, leaving the earth dark and lifeless, as described in Genesis 1:2.

God begins His plan of salvation

God recreated the earth and life on it in six days. He gave us physical bodies through which we could express ourselves on the earth in a physical three-dimensional plane. He made it possible for us to use our intelligence and raw materials to create a paradise on earth if we had the will to do so. Over a period of time we were to prove to all of creation and ourselves whether or not our way really was better than His. He would stay out of our affairs to a certain extent but He did raise up a people through whom He would speak to everyone on earth. This people would record His inspired word and their relationship with Him as an example of the actual result of obedience and disobedience.

He made the law of cause and effect an integral part of our everyday experience so we would experience first hand the results of our thoughts, words and actions. After all, we cannot really know anything unless we personally experience it. Before we fell we did not know what death was or pain, sickness, hardship, remorse, sadness, etc. We were given the gift of procreation so we could experience the joys and pains of parenthood and understand His own feeling for us as His children.

We would experience light and darkness and the difference between good and evil. We would experience the good and evil of human nature and experience the results of our own fallen nature. But at the same time His chosen people would stand as an example of how things could be even in our fallen state if we would just repent and turn to Him in obedience and trust. The record also showed the continual failure of unredeemed human nature to be able to form a workable society of peace and prosperity for every member. And man seemed to be unable or unwilling to continue in trust and obedience to Him even after solemnly agreeing to do so. Man was learning that without God he invariably descended ever lower. The Nazi holocaust is a recent example of this.

"Now the works of the flesh are manifest, which are these: Adultery, fornication, uncleanness, lasciviousness, idolatry, witchcraft, hatred, variance, emulations, wrath, strife, seditions, heresies, envyings, murders, drunkenness, revellings, and such like, of the which I tell you before, as I have also told you in time past, that they which do such things shall not inherit the Kingdom of God" (Gal. 5:19-21).

Christ provides salvation

Finally, at the predicted time as recorded in the pages of Scripture, God came to His chosen people as their Messiah to shed His blood for the sins of the world (Rom. 3:24,25; Eph. 1:7; Col. 1:14; 1 John 1:7). As Messiah God the Son incarnated in the flesh as man. He was at once the Son of Man, and the Son of God. As Son of Man He became our Kinsman Redeemer as mentioned earlier in Scripture (Lev. 25:24,25,47-49; Ruth 3:9,12; 4:1,3,6,8,14 (NIV)). His primary mission was to shed His blood and die for our sins, to pay our penalty for us. He also established His church on earth which was composed of those who accepted His offer of redemption by repenting for the forgiveness of their sins in His name thereby receiving the gift of the Holy Spirit (Acts 2:38) Who would guide and help them in their new resolve to trust and obey Him.

Christ to establish His kingdom on earth

He returned to Heaven to receive His crown (Lk. 19:12-27), leaving His church to occupy and spread the Gospel of the coming Kingdom of Heaven. His Kingdom had been established at His first coming as a beach-head, but at a pre-determined time in the future He would return, and with a rod of iron destroy all man's governments and take over the reigns of government and rule the world for a thousand years.

He did not reveal the exact day and hour of His second coming, but in Matthew 24, He gave a general outline and told us to watch for certain things which would precede His coming. These included increasing deception, wickedness, wars and rumors of war, famines, sickness and earthquakes. Other indicators are found in Acts 15:16-18; Romans 9:28; 2 Thessalonians 2:1-4,8-12;

1 Timothy 4:1; 2 Timothy 3:1-7; 4:3,4; 2 Peter 3:3-13; Revelation 17:8,9,12,13.

There are some who believe Christ will return after 6000 years because of a prediction in a non-biblical book, the *Epistle of Barnabas*. Most Christian scholars agree that creation week was about 4000 B.C. If they are right, then A.D. 2000 marks the end of the six days of man and the beginning of Christ's Kingdom of Heaven on earth. That did not happen, but it is possible the starting date is wrong. Or who knows, maybe the Jewish calendar is correct and the year is now really 5773 and we still have 227 years to go. Down through the centuries there have been numerous predictions about the second coming of Christ. So far the failure rate remains 100%!

The rapture

Most Bible students think the church will be "raptured" out of the earth before the great tribulation, which is supposed to occur during the last seven years before Christ's return. This would require a secret rapture about which the Bible seems to be totally silent. Instead, Christ's second coming seems to be predicted to occur after the great tribulation:

> "And I saw thrones, and they sat upon them, and judgment was given unto them: and I saw the souls of them that were beheaded for the witness of Jesus, and for the word of God, and which had not worshipped the beast, neither his image, neither had received his mark upon their foreheads, or in their hands; and they lived and reigned with Christ a thousand years. But the rest of the dead lived not again until the thousand years were finished. This is the first resurrection" (Rev. 20:4,5).

Most people I have spoken to who believe in the pre-tribulation rapture also agree that the rapture and the first resurrection are simultaneous events, and yet we learn in Revelation 20:4,5 that the first resurrection takes place after the tribulation.

Jesus' second coming will be public

The idea of a pre-tribulation rapture requires a secret whisking away of the saints. Jesus seems to be anticipating just such a false doctrine when He warns His disciples:

> ➤ "Then if any man shall say unto you, Lo, here is Christ, or there, believe it not. For there shall arise false Christs, and false prophets, and shall shew great signs and wonders, insomuch that, if it were possible, they shall deceive the very elect. Behold, I have told you before. Wherefore if they shall say unto you, Behold, He is in the desert, go not forth. Behold, He is in the secret chambers, believe it not. For as the lightning cometh out of the east, and shineth even unto the west, so shall also the coming of the Son of man be" (Mt. 24:23-27).

> ➤ "For the Lord Himself shall descend from heaven with a shout, with the voice of the archangel, and with the trump of God, and the dead in Christ shall rise first" (1 Thes. 4:16).

> ➤ "Behold, He cometh with clouds, and every eye shall see Him, and they also which pierced Him. And all kindreds of the earth shall wail because of Him. Even so, Amen" (Rev. 1:7).

Scripture seems to be saying that Christ will return publicly with a lot of light, shouting and fanfare. This is hardly the picture of a secret rapture.

When Christ does return He will come with a huge cloud of the Heavenly angels and will be seen by everyone on earth (Mt. 24:30; Rev. 1:7). He will stand in the air and raise the dead saints to life. Then He will transform the living and resurrected saints from corruptible to incorruptible, from mortal to immortal (1 Cor. 15:52,53), "Then we which are alive and remain shall be caught up together with them in the clouds, to meet the Lord in the air, and so shall we ever be with the Lord" (1 Thes. 4:17).

Where will Jesus and His saints go after the rapture?

There are different ideas about what happens after the dead and living saints have risen to meet Christ in the air. Most say they go back to heaven for seven years until after the great tribulation. Christ then descends with His saints and rules the earth for a thousand years. Others say they all go to heaven and spend the thousand years there, leaving the earth without living humans. Satan is supposed to be bound for the thousand years on earth by the circumstance of having no one to tempt, since all the sinners are dead and the saints are in heaven.

I believe both these ideas are wrong. When Christ returns, transforms and raises the dead and living saints to meet Him in the air, we are told that they will ever be with the Lord (1 Thes. 4:17). So where will the Lord be after that? In Zechariah 14:4 we are told, ". . . His feet shall stand in that day upon the mount of Olives, which is before Jerusalem on the east." Is "that day" the same day He returns for His saints? In Zechariah 8:3 we are told, "Thus saith the LORD: I am returned unto Zion, and will dwell in the midst of Jerusalem, and Jerusalem shall be called a city of truth, and the mountain of the LORD of hosts the holy mountain."

Also:

> ➢ ". . . Ye men of Galilee, why stand ye gazing up into heaven? This same Jesus, which is taken up from you into heaven, shall so come in like manner as ye have seen Him go into heaven" (Acts 1:11).

> ➢ "Behold, the Lord cometh with ten thousands of His saints" (Jude 1:14).

I think these verses indicate that when the Lord returns and raises His transformed saints to meet Him in the air, he will then continue to descend with His angels and saints to the Mount of Olives from where He ascended. Here are some additional scriptures that seem to confirm that idea:

➤ "Yet have I set My King upon My holy hill of Zion. I will declare the decree the LORD hath said unto Me: Thou art my Son. This day have I begotten Thee. Ask of Me and I shall give Thee the heathen for Thine inheritance and the uttermost parts of the earth for Thy possession. Thou shalt break them with a rod of iron. Thou shalt dash them in pieces like a potter's vessel" (Ps. 2:6-9).

➤ "And it shall come to pass in the last days, that the mountain of the LORD'S house shall be established in the top of the mountains, and shall be exalted above the hills, and all nations shall flow unto it. And many people shall go and say, Come ye, and let us go up to the mountain of the LORD, to the house of the God of Jacob; and He will teach us of His ways, and we will walk in His paths. For out of Zion shall go forth the law, and the word of the LORD from Jerusalem. And He shall judge among the nations and shall rebuke many people. And they shall beat their swords into plowshares and their spears into pruninghooks. Nation shall not lift up sword against nation, neither shall they learn war any more" (Isa. 2:2-4).

➤ "But with righteousness shall He judge the poor and reprove with equity for the meek of the earth. And He shall smite the earth with the rod of His mouth, and with the breath of His lips shall He slay the wicked . . . They shall not hurt nor destroy in all My holy mountain, for the earth shall be full of the knowledge of the LORD as the waters cover the sea" (Isa. 11:4,9).

The kingdom of heaven on earth

These scriptures are talking about the coming Kingdom of Heaven. In the past I believed that about halfway through the great tribulation the saints are first taken to heaven where they participate in the wedding banquet of the Lamb referred to in

Revelation 19:7: "Let us be glad and rejoice, and give honour to Him, for the marriage of the Lamb is come, and His wife hath made herself ready." They then remain in heaven until the last and worse half of the great tribulation takes place. Then they come back to earth with Christ and His angels to establish the Kingdom of Heaven, where His Ten Commandment Law is enforced. The reason I no longer believe this is because of Revelation 20:4,5 where we are plainly told the first resurrection occurs after the tribulation.

I believe law enforcement is the chain with which Satan—the personification of the human spirit of rebellion—will be bound for the thousand years of Christ's Kingdom of Heaven on earth (Rev. 20:2). The unrighteous will no longer be given the choice of obedience. Obedience will be required, and disobedience will be swiftly punished with justice and mercy. In the Kingdom of Heaven there will be no injustice or corruption. "And in the days of these kings shall the God of heaven set up a Kingdom, which shall never be destroyed. And the Kingdom shall not be left to other people, but it shall break in pieces and consume all these kingdoms and it shall stand for ever" (Dan. 2:44).

When Christ returns, He will destroy all men's governments with His rod. This rod is an interesting weapon. In the twenty-third Psalm we read, ". . . Thy rod and Thy staff they comfort me." The LORD is portrayed here as the good shepherd who uses His rod to protect His sheep. His sheep find comfort in His rod but His enemies are smashed with it.

We are told in Amos and Acts that, "In that day will I raise up the tabernacle of David that is fallen, and close up the breaches thereof, and I will raise up his ruins, and I will build it as in the days of old, that they may possess the remnant of Edom, and of all the heathen, which are called by My name, saith the LORD that doeth this" (Amos 9:11,12; see Acts 15:16,17). This reference to a "remnant" indicates a lot of people will die in the battle of the nations against the LORD. Unredeemed men are not going to willingly give up their governments. That is why we hear so much about this rod of the LORD that will be used to smash resistance. "And out of His mouth goeth a sharp sword, that with it He should smite the nations, and He shall rule them with a rod of iron. And

He treadeth the winepress of the fierceness and wrath of Almighty God" (Rev. 19:15). The saints are also going to rule with Christ during the thousand years:

> ➤ "And he that overcometh, and keepeth My works unto the end, to him will I give power over the nations, and he shall rule them with a rod of iron. As the vessels of a potter shall they be broken to shivers, even as I received of My Father" (Rev. 2:26,27).

> ➤ "And hast made us unto our God kings and priests, and we shall reign on the earth" (Rev. 5:10).

These verses seem to contradict the notion that the saints will spend the thousand years in heaven while Satan and his demons roam an empty earth. The fact that Christ and His saints will rule the nations with a rod of iron indicates the people over whom they reign do not want to be ruled. This does not sound like heaven since everyone in heaven has voluntarily submitted to God's will. Notice these verses speak of the Kingdom *of* Heaven, not the Kingdom *in* Heaven.

During the thousand years Christ will demonstrate the contrast between man's government and God's government. The unrighteous will continue to be born, live and die as they do now. And they will continue to reincarnate. The difference will be the nature of the government under which they will live. The Kingdom of Heaven will be totally righteous and merciful. There will be no corruption or injustice. I believe the wicked will not be allowed to reincarnate at this time. They will be in ". . . outer darkness. There shall be weeping and gnashing of teeth" (Mt. 8:12). They won't be weeping and gnashing their teeth because of repentance but because they are not allowed to reincarnate and partake of the blessings of the Kingdom of Heaven and continue to practice their wickedness.

Scripture gives us several glimpses into the blessings of the Kingdom of Heaven. For one thing there will no longer be war; ". . . they shall beat their swords into plowshares, and their spears into pruning hooks. Nation shall not lift up sword against nation, neither shall they learn war any more" (Isa. 2:4). This verse also tells us people will be working and earning their living. Plowshares, after all, are used for plowing. This will not be a thousand year retirement program. Apparently animals will be changed:

> "The wolf also shall dwell with the lamb, and the leopard shall lie down with the kid, and the calf and the young lion and the fatling together, and a little child shall lead them. And the cow and the bear shall feed; their young ones shall lie down together, and the lion shall eat straw like the ox. And the sucking child shall play on the hole of the asp [cobra], and the weaned child shall put his hand on the cockatrice' [viper's] den. They shall not hurt nor destroy in all My holy mountain, for the earth shall be full of the knowledge of the LORD, as the waters cover the sea" (Isa. 11:6-9).

CHAPTER NINE

THE ANTICHRIST

Despite all the blessings of the Kingdom of Heaven, I believe most people will not believe Christ has really come. They will probably think He is another imposter who is more clever than those who preceded Him. After all, just before His coming, a false Christ will have come with signs and wonders claiming he was setting up a perfect world ruling government—a "new world order." He will have ruled the world for a few years and his rule will have become harsh and oppressive. He himself will have claimed to be Christ and/or God:

> "Let no man deceive you by any means, for that day shall not come except there come a falling away first, and that man of sin be revealed, the son of perdition, who opposeth and exalteth himself above all that is called God, or that is worshipped, so that he as God sitteth in the temple of God, shewing himself that he is God" (2 Thes. 2:3,4).

In symbolic language, he is described in Revelation as a beast rising up out of the sea:

> ➤ "And I stood upon the sand of the sea, and saw a beast rise up out of the sea, having seven heads and ten horns, and upon his horns ten crowns, and upon his heads the name of blasphemy . . . the dragon [Satan] gave him his power, and his seat, and great authority" (Rev. 13:1,2).

> ➢ "And there was given unto him a mouth speaking
> great things and blasphemies, and power was given
> unto him to continue forty and two months. And
> he opened his mouth in blasphemy against God,
> to blaspheme His name, and His tabernacle, and
> them that dwell in heaven. And it was given unto
> him to make war with the saints, and to overcome
> them. And power was given him over all kindreds,
> tongues, and nations. And all that dwell upon the
> earth shall worship him, whose names are not
> written in the book of life of the Lamb slain from the
> foundation of the world. If any man have an ear, let
> him hear" (Rev. 13:5-9).

In Revelation 13:11-18 we are told of another beast that works
with the first beast deceiving the world and forcing everyone to
obey the first beast and worship him. He does many miraculous
signs, and has an image made of the first beast that everyone is
forced to worship on pain of death. He also forces everyone to
receive a mark on his right hand or forehead. Without this mark no
one will be able to buy or sell.

There are a lot of ideas about what this mark might be such as a
tattoo or even a microchip imbedded under the skin in the forehead
and hand. The idea I find most acceptable is that it is changing the
Sabbath to Sunday. If the mark is forced on people against their
will by the government then how could they be condemned for
having it? It has to be something that people receive voluntarily. In
Daniel 7:25 we find:

> "And he shall speak great words against the most High,
> and shall wear out the saints of the most High, and think
> to change times and laws. And they shall be given into his
> hand until a time and times and the dividing of time."

The "he" here is referring to the antichrist, or Beast. This is
probably a government or institution that is, of course, headed up
by a person. Also, notice he will "think to change times and laws."

Embedded in the heart of the Ten Commandment Law is the Sabbath commandment, which is the only commandment that has to do with time.

The number of the beast

Consider the following question and answer from "Our Sunday Visitor" a Catholic Weekly, which can be found in the Bureau of Information, Huntington, Indiana, April 18, 1915:

> ➤ "What are the letters supposed to be in the Pope's crown, and what do they signify, if anything?"

> ➤ "The letters inscribed in the Pope's miter are these: VICARIUS FILII DEI, which is the Latin for 'VICAR OF THE SON OF GOD.' Catholics hold that the church, which is a visible society, must have a visible head. Christ before His ascension into heaven, appointed St. Peter to act as His representative . . . Hence to the Bishop of Rome, as head of the church, was given the title, 'VICAR OF CHRIST.'"

In Revelation 13:18 we read: "Here is wisdom. Let him that hath understanding count the number of the beast; for it is the number of a man; and his number is Six hundred threescore and six [666]." Those letters in the Pope's miter are in Latin. Some of the Latin letters also stand for numbers and are known as Roman numerals. When we add up those numbers we reach an interesting total:

V I C A R I U S	
5+1+100+0+0+1+5+0	=112
F I L I I	
0+1+50+1+1	= 53
D E I	
500+0+1	=501
TOTAL	**666**

Zero represents the letters with no numerical value. Greek and Hebrew also use letters to represent numbers and when the Latin Vicarius Filii Dei is translated into Greek and Hebrew we still come up with 666. So in three different languages we find the Pope's title equals 666!

I realize something similar to this has been done with a number of other individuals in history and this fact would seem to cast doubt on the reliability of using it to designate the Pope (or Papacy) as the beast or antichrist. But this is only one indicator describing this person and/or institution. When we include other indicators the Papacy seems to be the only entity that fulfills Bible prophecy.

The mark of the beast

In this regard, I find it interesting that in "A Doctrinal Catechism," (Catholic) page 174, we find the following question and answer:

> ➢ **Q**-Have you any other way of proving that the Church has power to institute festivals of precept?
>
> **A**-Had she not such power . . . she could not have substituted the observance of Sunday, the first day of the week, for Saturday, the seventh day, a change for which there is no Scriptural authority.

Also consider these statements, which are quoted from Ferraris' Ecclesiastical Dictionary (Catholic) Article, Pope:

> ➢ "The Pope is of so great dignity and so exalted that he is not a mere man, but as it were God, and the Vicar of God.
>
> ➢ "The Pope is of such lofty and supreme dignity that, properly speaking, he has not been established in any rank of dignity, but rather has been placed upon the very summit of all ranks of dignities...

> ➤ "He is likewise the divine monarch and supreme emperor and king of kings.

> ➤ "Hence the pope is crowned with a triple crown, as king of heaven and of earth and of the lower regions."

Remember, these statements are being made about a man, not God, where they really belong. Please don't think I am pointing all this out because I have some special hatred of the Roman Catholic Church. I recognize Roman Catholics from the top down sincerely believe that what they believe is true. I believe they are right where they agree with the Word of God and wrong where they don't. The same holds true of everyone else including me. All I am doing is pointing out that Scripture makes certain statements about the antichrist that seem to apply to the Roman Catholic Church.

This beast and/or antichrist mentioned in Scripture seems to be a world religious and political leader who rises out of the revived Roman Empire. The ten toes mentioned in Daniel 2:41-43 seem to be speaking of this revival:

> "And whereas thou sawest the feet and toes, part of potters' clay, and part of iron, the kingdom shall be divided. But there shall be in it of the strength of the iron, forasmuch as thou sawest the iron mixed with miry clay. And as the toes of the feet were part of iron, and part of clay, so the kingdom shall be partly strong, and partly broken. And whereas thou sawest iron mixed with miry clay, they shall mingle themselves with the seed of men; but they shall not cleave one to another, even as iron is not mixed with clay."

I believe we are seeing this prophecy being fulfilled as the Common Market nations of Europe are uniting and reforming along the same lines as the old Roman Empire. Here are some more interesting quotes from Roman Catholic literature:

➢ "The observance of Sunday by the Protestants is an homage they pay in spite of themselves to the authority of the Catholic church" (*Plain Talk for Protestants*, page 213).

➢ **Q**-How prove you that the church hath power to command feasts and holy days?

A-By the very act of changing the Sabbath into Sunday, which Protestants allow of, and therefore they fondly contradict themselves by keeping Sunday strictly, and breaking most other Feasts commanded by the same church.

Q-How prove you that?

A-Because by keeping Sunday they acknowledge the church's power to ordain feasts, and to command them under sin (Douay Catechism, page 59).

➢ "If the Bible is the only guide for the Christian then the Seventh-day Adventist is right, in observing the Saturday with the Jew . . . Isn't it strange, that those who make the Bible their only teacher, should inconsistently follow in this matter the tradition of the Catholic Church?" (*Question Box*, Ed., 1915, page 179).

➢ "The Catholic Church for over one thousand years before the existence of a Protestant, by virtue of her divine mission, changed the day from Saturday to Sunday" (*Catholic Mirror*, September 1893).

➢ "Reason and sense demand the acceptance of one or the other of these alternatives; either Protestantism and the keeping holy of Saturday or Catholicity and the keeping holy of Sunday. Compromise is impossible." (Card. Gibbins, in *Catholic Mirror*, Dec. 23, 1893).

➤ "Of course the Catholic Church claims that the change was her act . . . And the act is a MARK of her ecclesiastical authority in religious things" (H.F. Thomas, Chancellor of Cardinal Gibbons).

So the Catholic Church itself claims Sunday keeping as a MARK. This sounds like another clue to the identity of the Antichrist. I believe the evidence points to the Papacy as the person of the Beast, or Antichrist. Probably the European Common Market nations will be headed up by the Papacy and will be in fact the revived Roman Empire. Or perhaps the Pope of that time could be the real power and influence behind a more visible world leader. Only when the Antichrist sits in the temple of God in Jerusalem, declaring himself to be God and demanding worship, will he be revealed as the "man of sin" predicted in Scripture (2 Thes. 2:3,4).

During the Middle Ages, the Catholic Church had a monopoly on religion and political power in Europe, and from the fourth century enforced Sunday keeping and made Sabbath keeping a crime punishable by death.

But what about this mark being in the forehead or the hand? (Rev. 14:9). If we accept something and believe in it, we could say it is in our mind, represented by our forehead. If we don't necessarily believe in it, but just go along with it as a matter of convenience, we could say we are going along with it because it is handy or convenient. This mark has been around since the fourth century, and has spread to the protestant churches. Perhaps these churches are the image of the Beast referred to in Revelation 13:14. The protestant churches are descendents of the Roman Catholic Church. When they left the Catholic Church, they retained the man made tradition of Sunday keeping, accepting the Catholic excuse that God wanted Sunday to replace the Sabbath because Sunday keeping commemorated Christ's resurrection. But Christ says:

". . . this people honoureth Me with their lips, but their heart is far from Me. Howbeit in vain do they worship Me, teaching for doctrines the commandments of men" (Mk. 7:6,7).

Notice Christ is worshipped in vain when His worshippers keep men's commandments instead of God's.

Mother of harlots

In Revelation, we are told about a woman sitting on a scarlet colored beast:

> "...and I saw a woman sit upon a scarlet coloured beast, full of names of blasphemy, having seven heads and ten horns. And the woman was arrayed in purple and scarlet colour, and decked with gold and precious stones and pearls, having a golden cup in her hand full of abominations and filthiness of her fornication. And upon her forehead was a name written, MYSTERY, BABYLON THE GREAT, THE MOTHER OF HARLOTS AND ABOMINATIONS OF THE EARTH" (Rev. 17:3-5).

This passage goes on to explain what this symbology means: "And here is the mind which hath wisdom. The seven heads are seven mountains [hills], on which the woman sitteth" (Rev. 17:9). Rome sits on seven hills. Could the woman—the "mother"—be the Roman Catholic church? Could her offspring—the "harlots"—be the protestant churches? Some statements by protestant leaders seem to confirm this possibility:

> ➢ "Resolved that the Sabbath [Sunday] is a sign between God and man, and its reverent observance a MARK of the nation whose God is Jehovah" (National Reform Convention, September 1887).

Many churches refer to Sunday as the Christian Sabbath:

> "We hereby agree . . . that such Sabbath [Sunday] observance laws for the District of Columbia may be looked upon not only as model Sabbath observance laws for America, but as model Sabbath observance laws for the rest of the world" (*Christian Statesman*, September 1927).

> "We insist upon the challenge, 'All must rest, that all may.' We stand by the battle cry, 'No special privileges and no seventh day subsidy.' If the Sabbath [Sunday] laws need adjusting to 'works of necessity' of the twentieth century, we will alter and adjust them ourselves" (*Christian Statesman*, March 1927).

One world government and religion

Some people would like to see Sunday keeping enforced again. Even without formal enforcement there is at this time an informal enforcement against many of those who obey God's Sabbath Commandment. Many Sabbath keepers find it difficult to find employment. I believe when conditions are right Sunday keeping will be enforced again by the government. Probably when crime, the economy and other problems such as corruption in government reach a certain point people are going to demand drastic changes and there will come on the scene a man with a plan, which will sound so reasonable that most people will embrace him as the answer to their problems just as Adolph Hitler was accepted in Germany during hard times.

But this will probably be a world leader addressing a world problem. I believe he will be the Pope. Already we are hearing about a "new world order." There seems to be a concerted effort to unify the world under one government and religion. The United Nations wants its own army to enforce its laws and there are congressmen and others in this country as well as leaders in other countries who support a stronger U.N. This will probably be presented as the answer to the age-old problem of continuous war and want. Bring all people together under one government and religion and there will be world peace and prosperity at last.

This all sounds great, but those who are familiar with Bible prophecy will recognize this as the predicted coming of the Antichrist. He will bring peace and prosperity for a few years, but being human, he will also bring tyranny and misery on a scale unmatched in history. It seems he will make a peace treaty between Israel and her enemies and will guarantee Israel's security. When her enemies attack Israel this world leader will bring the combined military power of the renewed Roman Empire against these attackers and defeat them. Daniel 11:40 seems to be referring to this encounter:

> "And at the time of the end shall the king of the south push at him: and the king of the north shall come against him like a whirlwind, with chariots, and with horsemen, and with many ships; and he shall enter into the countries, and shall overflow and pass over."

Israel will of course welcome this victorious world leader as its savior, but then he will enter the holy temple, declare himself to be God and demand to be worshiped. This sounds a lot like the Pope to me since he is already revered and worshipped worldwide by most of his followers as if he were God, as shown above, quoting from their own literature. Notice that there will be a temple in Jerusalem that has yet to be built. When this "son of perdition" sits in the temple demanding worship, the Jews and Christians will resist his demands and will be persecuted as a result. There are many who believe all the Christians will have been raptured by this time. I don't think so. As noted earlier Scripture seems to teach that Christians will go through the tribulation. But God is just as able today to protect His saints as He was when He protected Shadrach, Meshach, and Abednego from the fiery furnace and Daniel from the lions (Dan. 3:26,27; 6:22).

CHAPTER TEN

WHEN WILL CHRIST RETURN?

When Jesus is explaining to His disciples when He will return, in answer to their question, He tells them:

> "But of that day and that hour knoweth no man, no, not the angels which are in heaven, neither the Son, but the Father" (Mk. 13:32).

Then He gives them some signs to watch for and tells them:

> "Watch therefore, for ye know not what hour your Lord doth come" (Mt. 24:42).

Earlier in the same chapter He gave them more signs to watch for so it seems clear that even though we cannot know the day or hour we have been given some signs to watch for. Isn't it interesting that Jesus told His disciples to watch for signs that would appear near the time of His second coming over two thousand years after they died? Did Jesus know His second coming would be so far in the future, or did He think He would return during their lifetime? Even though He did say, while He was in the flesh, even He did not know the day or hour of His return, would He have made such a statement if He wasn't sure they would be alive on earth in the flesh to watch for and see the signs He described? As explained earlier, this could be another clue that reincarnation is a fact? How else could His disciples be in the flesh on earth watching for the signs of His return unless they reincarnated at that time?

A visible coming

In Matthew 24:30,31 Jesus links His coming with a loud trumpet call:

> "And then shall appear the sign of the Son of man in heaven. And then shall all the tribes of the earth mourn, and they shall see the Son of man coming in the clouds of heaven with power and great glory. And He shall send His angels with a great sound of a trumpet, and they shall gather together His elect from the four winds, from one end of heaven to the other."

Notice that all the nations of the earth will see Jesus coming. This seems to rule out a secret rapture. His second coming will be heralded by a loud trumpet call and He is coming for, not with, His elect.

The last trumpet

We are given the same message in 1 Corinthians 15:51,52:

> "Behold, I shew you a mystery: We shall not all sleep, but we shall all be changed in a moment, in the twinkling of an eye, at the last trump. For the trumpet shall sound, and the dead shall be raised incorruptible, and we shall be changed."

Here we are again told about a trumpet and we are told this trumpet will be the last trumpet. Also notice Jesus comes for, not with, His saints. I would also like to remind you that Paul uses the word "we" here which tells me he expected to be alive on earth in the flesh at Christ's second coming along with those to whom he was writing. And since he was writing under the inspiration of the Holy Spirit, then the Holy Spirit is telling us Paul and those to whom he was writing, would be alive on earth in the flesh at the second coming of Jesus.

In 1 Thessalonians 4:15-17 we read:

> "For this we say unto you by the word of the Lord, that we which are alive and remain unto the coming of the Lord shall not prevent [precede] them which are asleep. For the Lord Himself shall descend from heaven with a shout, with the voice of the archangel, and with the trump of God, and the dead in Christ shall rise first. Then we which are alive and remain shall be caught up together with them in the clouds, to meet the Lord in the air, and so shall we ever be with the Lord."

There's that trumpet call again. Also we again see that this is the time Jesus comes for His saints, not with them. And again, as mentioned earlier, we see another indication that reincarnation is a fact since Paul and those to whom he is writing will, "by the word of the Lord," be alive on earth in the flesh at His second coming.

The first seal rider

In the sixth chapter of Revelation, the Great Tribulation begins with the opening of the first of seven seals releasing a white horse and its rider who has a bow and a crown and rides out as a conqueror bent on conquest. There is some debate as to who this rider is. Some think he is Jesus. Others think he is the false church conquering by deception and twisting the truth. I agree with this second viewpoint because when Jesus was explaining to His disciples what to watch out for in the last days, the first thing He mentioned was deception: "And Jesus answered and said unto them:

> "Take heed that no man deceive you. For many shall come in My name saying, I am Christ, and shall deceive many" (Mt. 24:4,5).

Also, in context, this first rider is followed by a rider who takes peace from the earth and makes men kill each other (Rev. 6:4), followed by a rider who brings shortages of food, followed by a rider who brings death by sword, famine and plague, and by the wild beasts of the earth (vs. 8). It seems unlikely these destructive conditions would follow the second coming of Christ. When I see what has been going on in the world for the last few decades I wonder if those first four seals have already been opened and those four horsemen are riding throughout the earth now.

The trumpet seals

And these are just the beginning. It gets progressively worse. These are just the opening of the first four of seven seals. When the seventh seal is opened, seven angels are given seven trumpets. As each angel sounds his trumpet, tribulation judgment is sent to earth in ever increasing severity until we come to the seventh trumpet: "And the seventh angel sounded, and there were loud voices in heaven saying, The kingdoms of this world are become the Kingdoms of our Lord, and of His Christ; and He shall reign for ever and ever" (Rev. 11:15).

A problem with the last trumpet

Notice that this seventh trumpet is also the last trumpet, not only in this series of seven trumpets but for the rest of Scripture. I used to believe this is the trumpet that Jesus and Paul were talking about that would sound at the second coming and if so, that would indicate that Jesus would come at about the middle of, or two-thirds through the tribulation.

I held this conclusion for several years until I noticed in Revelation 20:4,5 that the first resurrection takes place after the tribulation is over and just before the thousand year reign of Christ on earth. When I first saw this I had trouble reconciling it with the last trumpet that sounds *at* the seventh trumpet and is followed by seven more judgments before the tribulation ends. At first I thought the explanation might be that these verses are actually a summery of an earlier event that took place at the last trumpet but I could see no room in the text for such an explanation. What puzzled me was that Paul tells us that Christ will return *at* the last trumpet. That indicates the rapture would occur at the very moment of the sounding of that seventh trumpet.

When I checked the Greek word "en" which was translated "at" in the text, I found it could also mean "after." If that is what the Holy Spirit was actually saying then the prophecy would read: "Behold, I shew you a mystery; We shall not all sleep, but we shall all be changed in a moment, in the twinkling of an eye, [*after*] the last trump. For the trumpet shall sound, and the dead shall be raised incorruptible, and we shall be changed" (1 Cor. 15:51,52). Since Revelation 20:5 tells us the first resurrection occurs after the tribulation and after the last trumpet, I believe this is the correct translation. Most believers believe the resurrection takes place before the Great Tribulation, and they spend that time safely tucked away in heaven. One very popular reason given for this belief is they don't want to be here during the great tribulation. I can certainly relate to that but truth is not altered by what we want to believe, is it? Truth is the way things are regardless of what we believe.

However there is another problem with that seventh trumpet that occurs to me and that is the statement that: "The kingdoms of this world are become the Kingdoms of our Lord, and of His Christ; and He shall reign for ever and ever" (Rev. 11:15). That indicates that at the sounding of that seventh trumpet Christ immediately takes over the reigns of world government. The only problem with that view is the increasing severity of the seven bowls judgments following that trumpet. But they don't follow immediately. In verse 18 we learn: "And the nations were angry, and thy wrath is come, and the time of the dead, that they should be judged, and that thou shouldest give reward unto thy servants the prophets, and to the saints, and them that fear thy name, small and great; and shouldest destroy them which destroy the earth." This indicates that even though "The kingdoms of this world are become the Kingdoms of our Lord, and of His Christ," He will not return until after the seven bowl judgments, which appear to be a mopping up operation. Also, I believe those last judgments could be very swift, lasting only a week or so. So we should not confuse His taking over the reigns of world government with His actual return in victory. It reminds me a little of General Douglas MacArthur returning to the Philippines in World War II. He said he would return, and after the enemy was defeated he did return.

There are four chapters between the last trumpet and the seven bowls judgments after which, at last, there comes:

> ". . . a white horse, and He that sat upon him was called Faithful and True, and in righteousness He doth judge and make war. His eyes were as a flame of fire, and on His head were many crowns. And He had a name written that no man knew but He Himself. And He was clothed with a vesture dipped in blood, and His name is called The Word of God" (Rev. 19:11-13).

What a picture this is of Christ coming with ". . . the armies which were in heaven . . . clothed in fine linen, white and clean" (vs. 14). This army is probably the saints returning from heaven with Jesus and His angels. Earlier, in Revelation 19:6-8, we read:

> "And I heard as it were the voice of a great multitude, and as the voice of many waters, and as the voice of mighty thunderings saying, Alleluia! For the Lord God omnipotent reigneth. Let us be glad and rejoice, and give honour to Him, for the marriage of the Lamb is come, and His wife [the church] hath made herself ready. And to her was granted that she should be arrayed in fine linen, clean and white; for the fine linen is the righteousness of saints."

CHAPTER ELEVEN

THE MILLENNIUM AND BEYOND

When Jesus returns, He establishes His rule over the whole world and reigns for a thousand years. We are told in Revelation 20:2,3 that at the beginning of the Millennium Satan is seized, bound and thrown into the Abyss where he will be kept for the duration of the thousand years. After the Millennium he is to be freed for a short time.

Satan bound for a thousand years

If I am right that Satan is the symbolic personification of man's spirit of rebellion against God then it is possible that the binding of Satan in the Abyss represents the enforcement of God's Law upon disobedient and rebellious mankind. At present He does not enforce His Ten Commandment Law. He is not making us obey them. This does not mean He does not require obedience nor does it mean there is no penalty for disobedience. It is still true that sin is the transgression of the Law (1 John 3:4) and the wages of sin is death (Rom. 6:23). I believe the Law referred to in 1 John 3:4 is the Ten Commandment Law, which is the only law in all of Scripture that consistently carries the death penalty and is associated with sin. Most believers would prefer to believe the Ten Commandment Law ended at the cross but there are too many times after the cross that this idea is found to be false. One example is found in James 2:10,11:

"For whosoever shall keep the whole law and yet
offend in one point, he is guilty of all. For He that said,
Do not commit adultery said also, Do not kill. Now if
thou commit no adultery, yet if thou kill, thou art become
a transgressor of the law."

Adultery and murder are two of the Ten Commandments, so
this must be the law James was writing about. James wrote this at
least twenty years after the cross. Notice he says "whosoever shall
keep the whole law and yet offend in one point, he is guilty of
all." The whole law would include all of the Ten Commandments,
wouldn't it?

The chain of law enforcement

Today we can obey or not as we choose. Unfortunately most
people choose disobedience. When Jesus returns and rules the
earth, disobedience will not be allowed. Satan—the symbolic
personification of our spirit of rebellion—will be bound by law
enforcement, symbolically represented by the "great chain"
mentioned in Revelation 20:1. Peace and prosperity will reign on
earth for a thousand years under the rule of Christ and His saints
(Rev. 20:6). Most of unredeemed humanity will submit to Christ's
rule only because they must, not because they choose to. This is
why we find Christ and His saints ruling with a rod of iron (Ps.
2:9; Rev. 2:27; 12:5; 19:15). If everyone obeyed voluntarily there
would be no need for a rod of iron to enforce obedience, would
there?

Ruling with a rod of iron

Revelation 20:5 says: "But the rest of the dead lived not
again until the thousand years were finished. This is the first
resurrection." Because of this verse, some imagine that only the
saints are resurrected and occupy the Kingdom of Heaven during
the Millennium. Since the saints do not have to be ruled with a rod
of iron, I am left with the picture of Christ and the saints ruling
over the unredeemed who are allowed to incarnate during the

Millennium. Perhaps the rest of the dead referred to in verse five are the wicked dead. I see the unredeemed divided into two groups: the decent and the wicked. Most people are decent, productive, hard working, tax paying people who obey society's laws, but they are unredeemed sinners and therefore lost. "But we are all as an unclean thing, and all our righteousnesses are as filthy rags; and we all do fade as a leaf, and our iniquities, like the wind, have taken us away" (Isa. 64:6). Then there are those who find pleasure in deliberately hurting, destroying, stealing and killing (Pr. 2:14; 4:16; 6:18; 21:10). I believe these are the ones God classifies as the wicked. During the Millennium I believe the wicked will not be allowed to reincarnate: "The righteous shall never be removed but the wicked shall not inhabit the earth" (Pr. 10:30). They are the ones who will be left in outer darkness to weep and gnash their teeth (Mt. 8:12; 22:13; 24:51; 25:30; Lk. 13:28). They won't be weeping and gnashing their teeth because they are repentant, but because they are frustrated and furious at not being allowed to reincarnate and practice their wickedness. This is another example of the symbology of Satan being bound.

Satan freed

After the thousand years of Christ's rule, we are told that Satan will be released from his prison and will go out to deceive the nations of the earth: "And when the thousand years are expired, Satan shall be loosed out of his prison and shall go out to deceive the nations which are in the four quarters of the earth, Gog and Magog, to gather them together to battle, the number of whom is as the sand of the sea" (Rev. 20:7,8). I believe this is a picture of Christ removing law enforcement for a while.

Why would Christ stop enforcing His Ten Commandment Law? Perhaps He wants to demonstrate to all of His creation for the last time the fact that whenever mankind is left to its own devices, outside of God's will, it will always degenerate into lawlessness, unrighteousness and wickedness. He is demonstrating the truth of His evaluation of unredeemed human nature as He expressed it before the flood in Genesis 6:5: "And God saw that the wickedness of man was great in the earth, and that every imagination of the thoughts of his heart was only evil continually." And after the flood: ". . . for the imagination of man's heart is evil from his youth" (Gen. 8:21). And now, after a full thousand years of Christ's rule on earth—in which He reinstates Eden—He removes enforcement of His Ten Commandment Law to demonstrate to all creation for one last time the utter depravity of unredeemed human nature and to demonstrate why He must finally but reluctantly ". . . do His work, His strange work; and bring to pass His act, His strange act" (Isa. 28:21), judging and destroying all sin in the lake of fire.

Postmillennial rebellion

Without law enforcement the unredeemed will again begin to do what comes naturally to the unredeemed mind; "Because the carnal mind is enmity against God, for it is not subject to the law of God, neither indeed can be" (Rom. 8:7). At the same time the wicked will again be allowed to reincarnate and in their intensified frustration, hatred and rage against Christ for restraining them from reincarnating and practicing their wickedness for a thousand years they will organize the people of the earth to attack and try to overthrow Christ and His saints who will be living in Jerusalem.

Who exactly are all these people who will be so easily persuaded to try to overthrow Christ? I believe many of them will be unbelievers such as atheists, agnostics and followers of false religions not based on the Bible. The rest will be those who consider themselves to be Christians but have never submitted to Christ as their LORD in repentance and obedience to His Ten Commandment Law. They are believers, but not Christians. Christians are always believers but believers are not always Christians. Even demons are believers: "Thou believest that there is one God; thou doest well. The devils also believe and tremble" (Jas. 2:19). In Matthew 7:21-23, Jesus said:

> "Not every one that saith unto Me, Lord, Lord, shall
> enter into the Kingdom of Heaven, but he that doeth the
> will of My Father which is in heaven. Many will say to
> Me in that day, Lord, Lord, have we not prophesied in

Thy name, and in Thy name have cast out devils, and in
Thy name done many wonderful works? And then will I
profess unto them, I never knew you. Depart from Me,
ye that work iniquity [practice lawlessness]."

They probably won't even believe Christ is Christ because the
details of His coming and reign on earth won't coincide with their
erroneous preconceptions. For example many believe they will be
raptured to Heaven before the great tribulation. When they are not
they will believe Christ is just another imposter like the Antichrist,
but more clever, utilizing modern technology to deceive them.
It won't occur to them that they really are *not* Christians. This
happened when Christ came the first time. The theologians of that
day did not recognize Him and in harmony with the Roman pagans
of that day finally had Him executed because He did not agree with
their erroneous preconceptions.

This time, when they try to kill Christ, ". . . fire came down
from God out of heaven, and devoured them" (Rev. 20:9). Then
Satan is thrown into the lake of fire. This may be a picture of man's
disobedient nature finally being purged and destroyed. Verses
eleven through fifteen describe the great white throne judgment.
All the dead are standing before it. The sea, death and hell (or
Hades, both of which means the grave) all give up the dead, after
which death and hell are also thrown into the lake of fire, which
is described as the second death. Incidentally, if hell is the lake of
fire, as many believe, then the statement that hell is thrown into the
lake of fire doesn't make sense, does it?

The second death

I have been assured by many that this phrase "the second
death" found in Revelation 20:14 proves that reincarnation cannot
be true since the first death is the death of our physical body. We
must remember that Revelation is filled with symbology. I believe
the first death is our series of deaths in the flesh. If reincarnation is
true we survive the death of our bodies anyway, don't we?

> "And fear not them which kill the body but are not
> able to kill the soul, but rather fear Him which is able to
> destroy both soul and body in hell" (Mt. 10:28).

The second death in the lake of fire is the last and final death of the flesh and the soul from which there is no return.

Before the throne, books are opened, and then "another book is opened, which is the book of life" (Rev. 20:12). "If anyone's name was not found written in the book of life he was thrown into the lake of fire" (vs. 15). Could the books (plural) mentioned here be the books of the Bible from which people will be judged worthy or unworthy to have their names written in the book of life?

The last chance

It seems to me that something happens between the destruction of that great army of rebels and the Great White Throne judgment. All those rebels are brought back to life after being destroyed by fire from heaven (Rev. 20:9,12,13). I believe they will then be given a review of the history of mankind from the time they first rebelled in heaven, were cast down to the earth and were given God's plan of salvation, which included the opportunity to experience the results of their rebellion in different lifetimes through the vehicle of reincarnation. Their lives will be compared to the model and instructions that were made available to them in the books of the Bible. They will be reminded of how they experienced the death of loved ones, and their own deaths and how they were given God's plan for their salvation from the consequences of their sins—eternal death. They will be reminded that because Christ came down and died in their place for their sins they could repent of their sins—their transgressions against the Ten Commandment Law (1 John 3:4)—and by God's grace be freely forgiven and receive the gift of the Holy Spirit and eternal life (Acts 2:38).

I believe Jesus is alluding to this time when he said:

> ➤ "Verily I say unto you, It shall be more tolerable for Sodom and Gomorrha in the day of judgment, than for that city" (Mark 6:11)

> ➤ "But it shall be more tolerable for Tyre and Sidon at the judgment, than for you" (Luke 10:13).

According to Jesus the people of Sodom, Gomorrha, Tyre and Sidon will not only be standing at the Judgment but they will be treated more tolerably than some others.

All those standing at the Judgment never knew the truth because they had not heard it. They had heard different variations of counterfeits of the truth. God made the truth available but most people did not want to believe it and apply it "Because the carnal mind is enmity against God, for it is not subject to the law of God, neither indeed can be" (Rom. 8:7). They preferred to live their way instead of God's way, while all the time convincing themselves they were indeed living God's way and were qualified for salvation. "There is a way which seemeth right unto a man, but the end thereof are the ways of death" (Pr. 14:12; 16:25).

Two roads

In the Sermon on the Mount, Jesus tells us about two roads with two destinations:

> "Enter ye in at the strait gate, for wide is the gate and broad is the way that leadeth to destruction and many there be which go in thereat, because strait is the gate and narrow is the way which leadeth unto life, and few there be that find it" (Mt. 7:13,14).

Notice that there are many people on the broad road. Jesus does not say they found it; they are just naturally on it. Since "all have sinned and come short of the glory of God" (Rom. 3:23) it seems probable to me that we are all born on that broad way leading to destruction. The road that leads to life is narrow and few people find it. It seems that in order to find the road leading to life one has to diligently seek for it. Jesus said ". . . seek and ye shall find" (Mt. 7:7).

According to recent statistics 14% of the world's population is listed as atheist or non-religious. Of the other 86% that are listed as religious, 33% consider themselves to be Christians. This is the highest percentage of all the other groups. The next largest group is Islam with 22%. All of these people except the nonreligious and the atheist probably believe they are on the road that leads to life. The atheists believe there is no after life at all and they are not on either road. Do any of these people believe they are on the road to destruction? I doubt it! This high percentage of Christians seems to contradict Christ. Either most people who believe they are Christians are honestly mistaken or Christ made a false statement in Matthew 7:13,14. According to Him, few people find the narrow road to life but most people are on the broad road to destruction. Everyone is on one of these two roads, so if Jesus is correct, and I believe He is, then most people who now believe they are Christians are sincerely mistaken.

God makes sure everyone knows the truth

After their destruction by fire from heaven it appears the rebels are resurrected. No doubt Christ now has their undivided attention. They no longer doubt that He is indeed Christ and God. He reviews with them the entire history of mankind's attempt to create heaven on earth without God in contrast with the thousand years of His rule on earth. He sees to it that they know the truth and they know they know the truth. Then they will be given time to either accept salvation and apply it in their lives or reject it. How much time this will take is not given, although I believe we may have a hint in Isaiah 65:20:

> "Never again will there be in it an infant who lives but a few days, or an old man who does not live out his years; he who dies at a hundred will be thought a mere youth; he who fails to reach a hundred will be considered accursed" (NIV).

I believe Christ will not condemn anyone to eternal death until he has learned the truth and has had an opportunity to apply it. "The Lord is not slack concerning His promise, as some men count slackness; but is longsuffering to us-ward, not willing that any should perish, but that all should come to repentance" (2 Pet. 3:9). Most of the rebels will submit to Christ as their LORD in repentance and obedience to His Ten Commandment Law. Until they do this He cannot be their savior (Acts 2:38; Heb. 5:9; Jas. 4:7). Incredibly, even after all this there will still be some who will refuse to submit to Christ as their LORD in repentance and obedience to His Ten Commandment Law. Perhaps after they learn the absolute truth and know they know the truth they will realize they would be miserable living in obedience to Christ. They would rather be dead if they cannot continue to pursue their own sinful, wicked interests. During the millennium they got a preview of how things would be and they did not like it. So they will be cast into the lake of fire where Satan, the beast, the false prophet, death, and Hades had been thrown. That looks like a pretty clean sweep to me. It also looks like a certain amount of symbology. Aren't the beast and false prophet symbolic? I believe Satan is symbolic. We are told these three symbolic beings will be tormented day and night forever and ever (Rev. 20:10).

Eternal torment?

Could there be some symbolism in the statement that they will be tormented day and night forever and ever? Notice that death and Hades are not included in this everlasting torment, nor are those whose names were not found in the Book of Life (Rev. 20:14,15) even though these three were also thrown into the lake of fire. Other scriptures tell us the lost will perish:

> "For God so loved the world that He gave His only
> begotten Son, that whosoever believeth in Him should
> not perish but have everlasting life" (John 3:16).

A distinction is made here between those who perish and those who have everlasting life. Since everlasting life is self-explanatory, isn't it reasonable to assume "perish" means just the opposite of everlasting life; that is, everlasting death, rather than everlasting life in torment in the lake of fire? In Ezekiel 18:4 we are told, ". . . the soul that sinneth, it shall die." The words "die" and "perish" don't mean the same as everlasting life, do they?

But there is another passage in Scripture that does seem to indicate that the lost will be tormented forever in the lake of fire. In Revelation 14:9-11 we read:

> "And the third angel followed them, saying with a loud voice, If any man worship the beast and his image, and receive his mark in his forehead, or in his hand, the same shall drink of the wine of the wrath of God, which is poured out without mixture into the cup of His indignation; and he shall be tormented with fire and brimstone in the presence of the holy angels, and in the presence of the Lamb. And the smoke of their torment ascendeth up for ever and ever, and they have no rest day nor night who worship the beast and his image, and whosoever receiveth the mark of his name."

If this really means eternal torment for the lost, then there seems to be a contradiction with John 3:16, Ezekiel 18:4 and the other scriptures I have mentioned. It could be said that smoke rises forever even though that which was burned up and caused the smoke has long since ceased to exist. The word "smoke" here could even be symbolic of the fact that the unrepentant perished and ceased to exist. The expression, "It went up in smoke" usually means whatever went up in smoke came to an end and ceased to exist. The last part of that verse revealing "and they have no rest day or night who worship the beast and his image, and whoever receives the mark of his name," sounds like a separate statement. There are no punctuation marks in the original manuscripts. An uninspired man added them hundreds of years later, so if we put a period in place of a comma after "for ever and ever," the rest of the verse could have been written as a separate sentence. People never find perfect rest and peace in Christ as long as they continue to refuse to submit to Him in repentance and obedience to His Ten Commandment Law.

Also notice in the last sentence in this passage there seems to be a switch to a universal statement that whoever receives the mark of the beast will be tormented day and night. There is no mention here of forever and ever. Perhaps we are merely being reminded here that those who accept the mark of the beast (which I believe is Sunday keeping in place of the Sabbath) will experience torment because even though they believe they are doing God's will, in fact they are in direct disobedience to Him. Their torment is their guilty conscience pricked by the prompting of the Holy Spirit. They also experience the physical torment, which is the natural result of their rebellion. "Be not deceived, God is not mocked, for whatsoever a man soweth, that shall he also reap" (Gal. 6:7).

Who are God's saints?

Revelation 14:12 seems to lend credibility to this viewpoint: "Here is the patience of the saints; here are they that keep the Commandments of God, and the faith of Jesus." Notice the saints are identified as those who obey God's Commandments. Saints are referred to throughout the Word of God as those who are in submission to Him as LORD in repentance and obedience to His Ten Commandment Law and therefore belong to Him. Revelation 12:17 says the same thing: "And the dragon was wroth with the woman, and went to make war with the remnant of her seed, which keep the Commandments of God, and have the testimony of Jesus Christ." Obeying God's Commandments means obeying all ten of them His way, not ours. God's Ten Commandment Law is an indivisible unit. It cannot be added to nor subtracted from, according to James 2:10: "For whosoever shall keep the whole law, and yet offend in one point, he is guilty of all." Revelation 14:9-11 speaks of the consequence of receiving the mark of the beast as opposed to keeping God's Commandments.

God's sign for His saints

Which day we keep and how we keep it doesn't seem to concern too many people, but all through Scripture God takes it very seriously and for us it is a matter of eternal life or death. Sabbath keeping is God's sign or mark identifying those who truly belong to Him:

> "Speak thou also unto the children of Israel saying, Verily My Sabbaths ye shall keep, for it is a sign between Me and you throughout your generations, that ye may know that I am the LORD that doth sanctify you . . . Wherefore the children of Israel shall keep the Sabbath, to observe the Sabbath throughout their generations, for a perpetual covenant. It is a sign between Me and the children of Israel for ever, for in six days the LORD made heaven and earth, and on the seventh day He rested and was refreshed" (Ex. 31:13,16,17. Also see Ezek. 20:12,20).

There are those who claim that these verses are telling us the Sabbath is only for the Jews. Notice in the passage above that God refers back to creation week when He rested and sanctified the seventh day and made it holy. He did this over two thousand years before the existence of a Jew. Also, God said the Sabbath is for everyone, not just the Jews:

> "Also the sons of the stranger that join themselves to the LORD to serve Him and to love the name of the LORD to be His servants, every one that keepeth the Sabbath from polluting it, and taketh hold of my covenant, even them will I bring to My holy mountain and make them joyful in My house of prayer . . . for Mine house shall be called an house of prayer for all people" (Isa. 56:6,7).

Jesus confirmed this fact when He said, "The Sabbath was made for man . . ." (Mk. 2:27). The word "man" here means mankind not just the Jews. God told the Israelites the Sabbath was a sign between Him and them because He had chosen them to be the people He would work with and use as an example to the world. They would preserve His written revelation to the world and the history and the consequences of their obedience and disobedience. The Sabbath was and is a sign identifying those who truly belong to Him. The Holy Bible is the only religious book on earth that claims the God of creation is the author, and to prove that claim, He gives us the Sabbath, which is the last thing He created on creation week. Those who worship a god of a different holy day are not worshipping the only true God of creation.

A popular teaching today is that the Ten Commandments ended at the cross but were reinstated with the exception of the Sabbath day. It is claimed that since the Sabbath Commandment is not repeated in the New Testament we no longer have to keep it. I believe this teaching is in error. In the first place the laws of the Old Testament were divided into the ceremonial law and the moral law. The ceremonial law, with its animal sacrifices, did end at the cross because it prophesied the coming of the true sacrificial Lamb of God—Christ. The moral law is referred to as being perfect and eternal: "The Law of the LORD is perfect, converting the soul...The works of His hands are verity and judgment; all His Commandments are sure. They stand fast for ever and ever, and are done in truth and uprightness" (Ps. 19:7; 111:7,8). Also, the idea that the Sabbath Commandment is not found in the New Testament is not true. Consider Hebrews 4:9: "There remains, then, a Sabbath-rest for the people of God" (NIV).

Israel forever

There are some who are convinced that God gave up on Israel and transferred to Christians His "chosen people" status, but He says just the opposite:

> ➤ "For the LORD will not forsake his people for his great name's sake: because it hath pleased the LORD to make you his people" (1 Sam. 12:22).

➤ "Thus saith the LORD; If heaven above can be
measured, and the foundations of the earth searched
out beneath, I will also cast off all the seed of Israel
for all that they have done, saith the LORD...
Considerest thou not what this people have spoken,
saying, The two families which the LORD hath
chosen, he hath even cast them off? thus they have
despised my people, that they should be no more a
nation before them. Thus saith the LORD; If my
covenant *be* not with day and night, *and if* I have not
appointed the ordinances of heaven and earth; Then
will I cast away the seed of Jacob, and David my
servant, *so* that I will not take *any* of his seed *to be*
rulers over the seed of Abraham, Isaac, and Jacob: for
I will cause their captivity to return, and have mercy
on them" (Jer. 31:37; 33:24-26).

➤ "I say then, Hath God cast away his people? God
forbid...God hath not cast away his people which
he foreknew...(According as it is written, God hath
given them the spirit of slumber, eyes that they
should not see, and ears that they should not hear;)
unto this day...I say then, Have they stumbled that
they should fall? God forbid: but *rather* through
their fall salvation *is come* unto the Gentiles, for to
provoke them to jealousy...For if the firstfruit *be*
holy, the lump *is* also *holy*: and if the root *be* holy,
so *are* the branches. And if some of the branches be
broken off, and thou, being a wild olive tree, wert
graffed [grafted] in among them, and with them
partakest of the root and fatness of the olive tree;
Boast not against the branches. But if thou boast,
thou bearest not the root, but the root thee. Thou
wilt say then, The branches were broken off, that I
might be graffed in. Well; because of unbelief they
were broken off, and thou standest by faith. Be not
highminded, but fear: For if God spared not the
natural branches, *take heed* lest he also spare not

thee. Behold therefore the goodness and severity of God: on them which fell, severity; but toward thee, goodness, if thou continue in *his* goodness: otherwise thou also shalt be cut off. And they also, if they abide not still in unbelief, shall be graffed in: for God is able to graff them in again. For if thou wert cut out of the olive tree which is wild by nature, and wert graffed contrary to nature into a good olive tree: how much more shall these, which be the natural *branches*, be graffed into their own olive tree? For I would not, brethren, that ye should be ignorant of this mystery, lest ye should be wise in your own conceits; that blindness in part is happened to Israel, until the fulness of the Gentiles be come in And so all Israel shall be saved: as it is written, There shall come out of Sion the Deliverer, and shall turn away ungodliness from Jacob" (Rom. 11:1,2,8,11,16-26).

Lazarus and the rich man

The story of Lazarus and the rich man, seems to be undeniable proof that after death we immediately go to heaven and eternal bliss, or the lake of fire where we suffer eternal torment:

"There was a certain rich man which was clothed in purple and fine linen and fared sumptuously every day. And there was a certain beggar named Lazarus, which was laid at his gate full of sores and desiring to be fed with the crumbs, which fell from the rich man's table. Moreover the dogs came and licked his sores. And it came to pass that the beggar died and was carried by the angels into Abraham's bosom. The rich man also died and was buried, and in hell he lift up his eyes being in torments and seeth Abraham afar off and Lazarus in his bosom. And he cried and said, Father Abraham have mercy on me and send Lazarus that he may dip the tip of his finger in water and cool my tongue, for I am tormented in this

flame. But Abraham said, Son, remember that thou in
thy lifetime receivedst thy good things and likewise
Lazarus evil things, but now he is comforted and thou
art tormented. And beside all this, between us and you
there is a great gulf fixed, so that they which would
pass from hence to you cannot; neither can they pass to
us that would come from thence. Then he said, I pray
thee therefore father that thou wouldest send him to
my father's house, for I have five brethren; that he may
testify unto them lest they also come into this place of
torment. Abraham saith unto him, They have Moses and
the prophets, let them hear them. And he said, Nay father
Abraham, but if one went unto them from the dead they
will repent. And he said unto him, If they hear not Moses
and the prophets, neither will they be persuaded though
one rose from the dead" (Lk. 16:19-31).

Many who believe in eternal torment consider this story to be
historical narrative. Others believe it is a parable. If it is to be taken
literally it seems to conflict with Scripture. After death Lazarus
finds himself in Abraham's bosom and the rich man is in torment
in the flames of hell. The only reason the rich man is in torment is
because he was rich. The only reason Lazarus went to Abraham's
bosom is because he was poor. Nothing is said about their moral
positions. If this story is to be taken literally it has to be literal
throughout. Lazarus is taken bodily to Abraham's bosom. The rich
man is first buried before he appears in the fire so he must be in the
spirit, and yet he experiences the physical sensation of thirst and
the agony of the extreme heat of the fire. The saved and the lost are
separated by a great chasm, which cannot be crossed and yet they
can see each other and communicate.

Where is there any record in Scripture that Abraham has been
resurrected? If only the poor go to Abraham's bosom regardless of
their moral position then why was Abraham on the good side of
the chasm since he was a rich man? Why was there no judgment?
I thought the judgment and the lake of fire are still over a thousand
years in the future. There is no mention of heaven here. Since most
of humanity is poor, does this mean there is a huge mountain of poor

people somewhere piled on top of hapless Abraham? Perhaps this is Abraham's punishment for being rich. Do the poor have to spend eternity watching the rich suffering the agony of hell fire and listening to their screams? Is any of this in harmony with the rest of Scripture?

If we consider the context of this story we should begin at Luke 15:2: "And the Pharisees and scribes murmured, saying, This man receiveth sinners and eateth with them." Jesus answers them with a series of parables. The first is the parable of the lost sheep, followed by the parable of the lost coin, followed by the parable of the lost son. Then He tells the parable of the shrewd immoral manager. "And the Pharisees also, who were covetous, heard all these things and they derided Him" (Lk. 16:14). So He then tells the story of the rich man and Lazarus. Some say this has to be a true story of life after death because no parable contains a man's name. The premise here is a parable cannot contain a man's name. The assumption is that since no other parable contains a man's name, therefore that is the rule. Is that not a ridiculous reason for establishing a rule?

Jesus was telling a parable using as a basis an erroneous belief held and taught by the religious teachers about life after death. He was not teaching the reality about life after death. His point is found in the punch line in verse 31:

> "And he said unto him, If they hear not Moses and the prophets, neither will they be persuaded though one rose from the dead."

He was condemning the Pharisees for refusing to believe the plain teaching of the scriptures.

The state of the dead

There are two major beliefs allegedly based on the Bible concerning the state of the dead. The most popular is the belief that when we die the soul immediately goes to heaven or hell. The other is the belief that we stay dead in the grave until the resurrection. This is usually called soul sleep. Those who believe this believe the soul is just another word for the physical body and therefore nothing survives the death of the body because the body is the soul.

Obviously only one of these beliefs can be true. It is also possible that they could both be wrong. Both beliefs seem to contradict Scripture. In Matthew 14:26,27, Jesus' disciples saw Him walking on the water. They were terrified:

> "It is a spirit; and they cried out for fear. But straightway Jesus spake unto them, saying: Be of good cheer; it is I, be not afraid."

Evidently the disciples believed in ghosts and Jesus did not correct them.

After Jesus arose from the dead He appeared to His disciples in the upper room:

> "But they were terrified and affrighted and supposed that they had seen a spirit. And He said unto them, Why are ye troubled? and why do thoughts arise in your hearts? Behold My hands and My feet, that it is I Myself. Handle Me and see, for a spirit hath not flesh and bones as ye see Me have" (Lk. 24:37-39).

In both of these accounts, the disciples are expressing a belief in ghosts. Jesus does not correct His disciples by explaining that there are no ghosts. Instead He describes ghosts as not having flesh or bones. If there were no ghosts, doesn't it seem strange that He would not correct His disciples who He is about to send into the world to teach the truth? Instead He is confirming their belief in ghosts by actually giving a brief description of them.

The two popular beliefs about the state of the dead have one thing in common. They exclude the existence of ghosts. If the soul goes directly to heaven or hell at the death of the body, then it cannot appear on earth as a ghost. This is also true if the soul is sleeping in the grave. Both of these ideas contradict the fact that Scripture says ghosts exist. Some claim that demons masquerade as ghosts of departed loved ones. If ghosts are demons why did Christ and His disciples not refer to them as demons instead of spirits (ghosts)? I believe ghosts and demons are both disincarnate entities. The difference is the demons are wicked.

One objection I have heard from those who agree that there are ghosts but still want to cling to their beliefs that we either go straight to heaven or hell when we die, or we simply "sleep" in the grave, is we are not really given a definition of a ghost in these verses. They agree that the disciples believed in ghosts and Christ partially described them but they don't see any reason to believe these ghosts are disincarnate humans. If not, then what could they be? Two Greek words are used in these verses. In Matthew 14:26 (and also Mark 6:49) the word is *phantasma*, which means specter or spirit. In Luke 24:37,39 the word is *pneuma*, which means the human spirit or the rational soul. In both cases it seems clear to me that the disciples thought they saw disincarnate human spirits and that is what Jesus was describing.

Demons

Christ and His apostles spoke of demons—devils—several times in Scripture. What exactly is a demon? The popular belief is that demons are the fallen angels that followed Satan when he and they were thrown out of heaven down to the earth. In a sense I can agree with this idea. If I am right that Satan is a term given to describe unredeemed human nature then when we follow the spirit of rebellion and disobedience we are following Satan, as Jesus alluded to in Matthew 16:23 when rebuking Peter:

> "But he turned, and said unto Peter, Get thee behind me, Satan: thou art an offence unto me: for thou savourest not the things that be of God, but those that be of men."

So what are demons? I believe they are disincarnate entities who are still practicing the wickedness they practiced in the flesh. They are "ghosts" who are still intent on doing the evil they practiced in the flesh and sometimes actually succeed in possessing someone's body. This is usually only possible if the present qualified occupant of that body invites the disincarnate entity in by practicing certain occult methods such as Ouija boards, automatic writing, spiritualism, etc. This is why Edgar Cayce warned against these practices. This is probably also why God forbids them.

The "soul sleep" belief also contradicts Jesus' statement:

> "And fear not them which kill the body but are not able to kill the soul, but rather fear Him which is able to destroy both soul and body in hell." (Mt. 10:28).

We learn quite a lot in this statement about the state of the dead. Jesus is saying:

> ➤ The soul and the body are two separate and distinct entities.

> ➤ The soul survives the death of the body.

> ➤ Both the body and the soul are mortal and can be destroyed by God.

Also Jesus said:

> "But as touching the resurrection of the dead, have ye not read that which was spoken unto you by God, saying, I am the God of Abraham, and the God of Isaac, and the God of Jacob? God is not the God of the dead, but of the living" (Mt. 22:31,32 see also Mk. 12:27 and Lk. 20:38).

A new heaven and earth

After God has saved from the consequence of their sins those who are really repentant and really want to be saved, and are willing to submit to Jesus as their LORD in repentance and obedience to His will—the Ten Commandment Law, and after He has cleansed the earth of all sin with fire, then the Holy City, the new Jerusalem, comes down from heaven. The old earth and heaven are replaced by a new earth and heaven:

"And I saw a new heaven and a new earth, for the first heaven and the first earth were passed away and there was no more sea. And I John saw the holy city—new Jerusalem—coming down from God out of heaven prepared as a bride adorned for her husband" (Rev. 21:1,2).

God inspired Peter to give a graphic description of this event:

"But the heavens and the earth, which are now by the same word; are kept in store reserved unto fire against the day of judgment and perdition of ungodly men . . . But the day of the Lord will come as a thief in the night in the which the heavens shall pass away with a great noise and the elements shall melt with fervent heat. The earth also and the works that are therein shall be burned up . . . Looking for and hasting unto the coming of the day of God, wherein the heavens being on fire shall be dissolved, and the elements shall melt with fervent heat. Nevertheless we, according to His promise, look for new heavens and a new earth wherein dwelleth righteousness" (2 Peter 3:7,10,12,13).

Heaven in these passages means the atmosphere around the earth.

Sin eradicated forever

This earth will only know true and lasting peace, prosperity and joy when God through Christ finally burns up every last trace of sin. He forces no one to want to submit to Him as LORD. He forces no one to want to obey Him. Throughout history He has consistently urged, pleaded and invited us to submit to Him as our LORD in repentance and obedience to His Ten Commandment Law. Only those who truly want to submit to Him as their LORD will be saved. The choice is ours. Those who stubbornly cling to their sins will be burned up with their sins in the lake of fire. God does not want this to happen, but it will after all else has failed:

"Have I any pleasure at all that the wicked should die? saith the Lord GOD, and not that he should return from his ways and live? . . . For I have no pleasure in the death of him that dieth, saith the Lord GOD. Wherefore turn yourselves and live ye" (Ezek. 18:23,32).

In Exodus 34:6,7, God describes Himself this way:

"And the LORD passed by before him [Moses] and proclaimed, The LORD, The LORD God, merciful and gracious, longsuffering and abundant in goodness and truth, keeping mercy for thousands, forgiving iniquity and transgression and sin..."

I would like to live in eternity with that God, wouldn't you? Other scriptures indicate that His saints will eventually be free once again to roam throughout God's vast creation, experiencing things we cannot even begin to imagine at present:

> ➤ "But as it is written, Eye hath not seen nor ear heard, neither have entered into the heart of man the things which God hath prepared for them that love Him" (1 Cor. 2:9).

> ➤ "He that overcometh shall inherit all things; and I will be his God and he shall be my son" (Rev. 21:7).

At present we are confined to a physical, three-dimensional world. I believe there are many more dimensions in God's creation that may be as endless and eternal as He is. I look forward to that time and I hope to see you there.

SALVATION IN SUMMARY

CHAPTER TWELVE

GOD'S WAY OR YOURS—WHICH?

Sin is the transgression of God's Ten Commandment Law (1 John 3:4). I know 1 John 3:4 does not say "Ten Commandment Law." It says "Sin is the transgression of the Law." But if we consider that the ceremonial law ended at the cross several years before this was written, then what other law could John have been referring to that defines sin and therefore ends in death (Rom. 6:23) if not God's moral Ten Commandment Law?

God personally wrote the Ten Commandment Law on two stone tablets with His finger. This is the only part of the whole Bible that God personally wrote Himself rather than through others. This fact indicates the Decalogue is extremely important to God. In the Decalogue (Ex. 20:1-17) God says: "I am the LORD thy God which have brought thee out of the land of Egypt, out of the house of bondage:

I

Thou shalt have no other gods before Me

II

Thou shalt not make unto thee any graven image, or any likeness of any thing that is in heaven above, or that is in the earth beneath, or that is in the water under the earth. Thou

shalt not bow down thyself to them, nor serve them, for I the
LORD thy God am a jealous God, visiting the iniquity of the
fathers upon the children unto the third and fourth generation
of them that hate Me, and shewing mercy unto thousands of
them that love Me, and keep My Commandments

III

Thou shalt not take the name of the LORD thy God in vain,
for the LORD will not hold him guiltless that taketh His name
in vain

IV

Remember the Sabbath day, to keep it holy. Six days shalt
thou labour, and do all thy work. But the seventh day is the
Sabbath of the LORD thy God; in it thou shalt not do any
work; thou, nor thy son, nor thy daughter, thy manservant, nor
thy maidservant, nor thy cattle, nor thy stranger that is within
thy gates. For in six days the LORD made heaven and earth,
the sea, and all that in them is, and rested the seventh day.
Wherefore the LORD blessed the Sabbath day, and hallowed it

V

Honour thy father and thy mother that thy days may be
long upon the land which the LORD thy God giveth thee

VI

Thou shalt not kill

VII

Thou shalt not commit adultery

VIII

Thou shalt not steal

IX

Thou shalt not bear false witness against thy neighbour

X

Thou shalt not covet thy neighbour's house. Thou shalt not covet thy neighbour's wife, nor his manservant, nor his maidservant, nor his ox, nor his ass, nor any thing that is thy neighbour's."

Obeying God His way

If we disobey only one Commandment we are lawbreakers and therefore sinners (Jas. 2:10). If I repent of Sabbath breaking and continue breaking the Sabbath each week, have I really repented, or am I an unrepentant sinner and lost? We must keep God's Sabbath God's way. In the Sabbath commandment we are told to rest from our labor and not to cause any other person or animal to work. Does anyone keep the Sabbath God's way? There are some who correctly believe it should be kept on the seventh day from sundown Friday through sundown Saturday as the scriptures teach (Lev. 23:32). But then they drive to church risking accident or breakdown that would require people to work: the police, ambulance drivers, doctors, a wrecker, or a mechanic, etc. Starting and running the car is igniting a fire, which is forbidden on the Sabbath (Ex. 35:3). At home and church, they use electricity, gas, water, and the phone, thus requiring the utility workers to work on the Sabbath. We are required to rest on the Sabbath, not worship. Other Scriptures tell us to worship every day: "Pray without ceasing" (1 Thes. 5:17).

However in Leviticus 23:3 the Hebrews were told that the Sabbath day was to be a holy convocation "...in all your dwellings." The Hebrew word translated "convocation" may also be translated public meeting, rehearsal, assembly, calling, or reading. Since it is qualified by the words "in all your dwellings," then it could mean each family is to assemble in their homes on the Sabbath. If the Hebrews were being told to assemble publicly on the Sabbath they could easily have done so without breaking the Sabbath because they were all together in the wilderness. But after they went into the promised land and spread out, they could not assemble at the tabernacle, and later the temple in Jerusalem every Sabbath because of the distances, some of which were over one hundred miles, so each town built at least one synagogue—a sort of temple annex—where the people could gather for fellowship and Bible study on the Sabbath. It was the custom of Jesus to go there each Sabbath (Lk. 4:16).

Keeping the Sabbath God's way in our present fallen world is not always easy. Jesus kept the Sabbath and so did His apostles, even after the cross. But Jesus also made an exception in a life or death situation, or to do good, as He explained in Matthew 12:11,12, Mark 3:4 and Luke 13:15,16. He didn't say we should go out on the Sabbath day looking for good to do, but if there is an emergency, we can do good without transgressing the Sabbath. If a child is injured in front of my house on the Sabbath day, Jesus said I can do what I can to help him, rather than leaving him in the street until after the Sabbath is over. He said that we could even help an animal in an emergency on the Sabbath day without violation.

Jesus was confronted about the Sabbath many times by the authorities. Several times He explained why what He was doing did not transgress the Sabbath Commandment. Over the centuries the Jews had added around 300 rules to the Sabbath Commandment. What He did transgress was their unscriptural rules they had added to the Sabbath day. At one point He challenged the authorities to convict Him of sin and they remained silent (John 8:46). When He was on trial they were desperately seeking some charge they could accuse Him of to justify killing Him, but not once did they charge Him with Sabbath breaking, which would have justified the death penalty. Why not? Because they knew He was innocent of such a charge.

At no time during His ministry did Jesus ever say anything about changing the Sabbath to Sunday, or that it should be ignored. Instead He faithfully kept the Sabbath day and so did His disciples and followers before and after His death: "And they returned and prepared spices and ointments; and rested the Sabbath day according to the Commandment" (Lk. 23:56). Most believers believe Sunday is the Lord's Day, but there is no place in Scripture that makes such a claim. Instead, Scripture clearly says the Sabbath day is the Lord's Day:

> ". . . turn away thy foot from the Sabbath, from doing thy pleasure on My holy day . . ." (Isa. 58:13).

> "For the Son of man is Lord even of the Sabbath day" (Mt. 12:8).

If Christ is Lord of the Sabbath day, doesn't that make the Sabbath the Lord's day? The author of Hebrews makes this statement concerning Jesus:

"For where a testament *is*, there must also of necessity be the death of the testator. For a testament *is* of force after men are dead: otherwise it is of no strength at all while the testator liveth" (Heb. 9:16,17).

While Jesus was alive, He did not change the Sabbath to Sunday. After His death His testament was sealed and could not be legally altered. The widely held current belief that His disciples made the change to honor His resurrection is fiction to justify a man made tradition. For example, one time Paul went into the synagogue on the Sabbath day in Antioch and told the people that Jesus was the promised messiah. Apparently there were Jews and gentiles there because we are told: "And when the Jews were gone out of the synagogue, the Gentiles besought that these words might be preached to them the next sabbath" (Acts 13:42). Why did Paul not say; "Christians do not keep the Sabbath. You can hear the message tomorrow when we meet on the first day of the week"? Instead; "And the next sabbath day came almost the whole city together to hear the word of God" (vs. 44).

When was the crucifixion?

Once, the Pharisees asked Jesus for a sign proving He was the promised Messiah:

> "But he answered and said unto them, An evil and adulterous generation seeketh after a sign; and there shall no sign be given to it, but the sign of the prophet Jonas: For as Jonas was three days and three nights in the whale's belly; so shall the Son of man be three days and three nights in the heart of the earth" (Mt. 12:39,40).

Most scholars tell us the crucifixion was on Friday and the resurrection was on Sunday morning. That is only two days unless you count Friday and Sunday as whole days, which they insist is the case. Okay, that would make three days, but where are the three nights? You have Friday night and Saturday night and that is only two nights. But Jesus gave as a sign that He was the Messiah if He would be dead three days and nights. If he was not, then He made a false statement and He is not the Messiah and we are still in our sins and lost.

Why do scholars believe Jesus was crucified on Friday? Because scripture seems to say that:

> ➤ "And now when the even was come, because it was the preparation, that is, the day before the Sabbath…" (Mk. 15:42).

> ➤ "And that day was the preparation, and the sabbath drew on" (Lk. 23:54).

> ➤ "The Jews therefore, because it was the preparation, that the bodies should not remain upon the cross on the sabbath day, (for that sabbath day was an high day,) besought Pilate that their legs might be broken, and that they might be taken away" (John19:31).

It is true that Friday does precede Saturday, the Sabbath, every week. What the scholars fail to notice is the Jewish calendar also contains seven annual Sabbaths. Jesus and His disciples kept the Passover the night before His crucifixion. Since Jewish days begin at sunset, the Passover was also the day of His crucifixion in the afternoon. The next day was the first day of the Seven Days of Unleavened Bread and was an annual Sabbath day that would commence at sundown. That is why John calls it a "high day." The annual Sabbath days can fall on any day of the week like Christmas or Thanksgiving. So which day did this annual Sabbath day fall on? Here are a couple of verses that give us a clue:

➢ "And when the sabbath was past, Mary Magdalene, and Mary the mother of James, and Salome, had bought sweet spices, that they might come and anoint him" (Mk. 16:1).

➢ "And they returned, and prepared spices and ointments; and rested the sabbath day according to the commandment" (Lk. 23:56).

Do you notice an apparent contradiction there? First, we are told the women bought the spices after the Sabbath was past. Then we are told they prepared the spices and rested on the Sabbath. Either this is a contradiction, or there are two Sabbaths, one before they bought the spices and another after they prepared the spices. So we have an annual Sabbath, which occurred after Jesus was crucified and a weekly Sabbath with a day in between. So we can conclude that Jesus must have been crucified on a Wednesday and placed in the tomb before sunset, which began the annual Sabbath of the First Day of Unleavened Bread. The women could not buy the spices on a Sabbath day. On Friday, they were free to buy the spices and prepare them. Then came the weekly Sabbath and they rested. Early Sunday morning they were on their way to the tomb to finish properly anointing Jesus' body.

So the evidence seems to indicate that Jesus was crucified on Wednesday, placed in the tomb just before sunset, and in harmony with His prophecy, rose on Saturday just before sunset, 72 hours later—three days and three nights.

One objection I hear concerning a Saturday resurrection is found in Mark 16:9: "Now when Jesus was risen early the first day of the week, he appeared first to Mary Magdalene, out of whom he had cast seven devils." This verse seems to conflict with the idea that Jesus rose just before sunset on the Sabbath, three days and three nights after His crucifixion, as He predicted. First, we should remember that the original manuscripts had no punctuation. That was added centuries later and was not inspired. So the comma probably should be placed after "risen." Notice how that changes the meaning: "Now when Jesus was risen, early the first day of the week..." Second, there is reason to believe verses 9 through 20 were not part of the original manuscript since they do not appear in some of the most ancient manuscripts such as Codex Sinaiticus and Codex Vaticanus. When the women arrived at the tomb, it was empty because Jesus had risen earlier.

An ideal world

Assuming that in an ideal world, such as the Kingdom of Heaven where everyone obeys God, how would the Sabbath be obeyed? Since the utility workers would also be keeping the Sabbath holy we would have to turn off all our utilities one hour before sunset on Friday to give the utility workers time to get home for the Sabbath. After sunset Saturday we would have to wait one hour to give them time to return to work before turning on our utilities. The Sabbath would be spent at home unless there was a church within walking distance, which in an ideal world there would be since we would all be keeping the Sabbath holy. The churches would not use any utilities on the Sabbath. But what is God's definition of the church?

> ➤ "So we, being many, are one body in Christ, and every one members one of another" (Rom. 12:5).

> ➤ "Know ye not that your bodies are the members of Christ?" (1 Cor. 6:15).

➤ "Now ye are the body of Christ, and members in particular" (1 Cor. 12:27).

➤ "And hath put all things under His feet, and gave Him to be the head over all things to the church, which is His body, the fulness of Him that filleth all in all" (Eph. 1:22,23).

So the true church is the body of Christ composed of those who belong to Him. What we call the church is only a building where Christians gather for fellowship, encouragement, Bible study and worship. A Christian is always in church, wherever he may be since he belongs to Christ and is grafted into His body (Rom. 11:16-24). Also, remember what Jesus told the Samaritan woman:

"Woman, believe me, the hour cometh, when ye shall neither in this mountain, nor yet at Jerusalem, worship the Father. But the hour cometh, and now is, when the true worshippers shall worship the Father in spirit and in truth: for the Father seeketh such to worship him. God is a Spirit: and they that worship him must worship him in spirit and in truth" (John 4:21, 23,24).

What does it mean to worship God in spirit and truth? Jesus said:

"I am the way, the truth, and the life: no man cometh unto the Father, but by me" (John 14:6).

"God is not limited by time and space. When people are born of the Spirit, they can commune with God anywhere. Spirit is the opposite of what is material and earthly…Christ makes worship a matter of the heart. Truth is what is in harmony with the nature and will of God. It is the opposite of all that is false. Here the truth is specifically the worship of God through Jesus Christ. The issue is not where a person worships, but how and whom" (From The Nelson Study Bible, copyright 1997 by Thomas Nelson, Inc. Used by permission.).

Does love replace the Ten Commandments?

One objection I sometimes hear from those who do not want to obey God's Ten Commandment Law is that the two great love commandments of the New Covenant have replaced it. In answer to the question, "Which is the greatest commandment in the law?" Jesus answers:

> "And thou shalt love the Lord thy God with all thy heart, and with all thy soul, and with all thy mind, and with all thy strength. This is the first commandment, and the second is like, namely this: Thou shalt love thy neighbour as thyself. There is none other commandment greater than these" (Mk. 12:30,31).

Many people conclude that these two greatest commandments have replaced the Ten Commandments. We should remember that Jesus was quoting from the Old Testament. He quoted the first commandment from Deuteronomy 6:4,5. This was known to the Hebrews as the Shemá, which became the Jewish confession of faith and was recited by pious Jews every morning and evening. To this day it begins every synagogue service. The second commandment was quoted from Leviticus 19:18. Please notice that the Hebrews were also required to obey the Ten Commandments, which are in the Old Testament in Exodus 20. Disobedience carried the death penalty.

If the two greatest commandments did not replace the Ten Commandments in the Old Testament, why should we assume they replaced them in the New Testament? Jesus ended His answer with the statement:

> "On these two commandments hang all the Law and the prophets" (Mt. 22:40).

He did not say these two commandments replaced the law and the prophets, did He? How can these two commandments replace the Ten Commandments, which are described as being eternal? ". . . all his Commandments are sure. They stand fast for ever and ever, and are done in truth and uprightness" (Ps. 111:7,8). The Ten Commandments are also described as being perfect: "The law of the LORD is perfect, converting the soul" (Ps. 19:7). If something is perfect, can it be improved? Paul said, "Do we then make void the law through faith? God forbid: yea, we establish the law" (Rom. 3:31). In context, Paul is talking about the Ten Commandment Law. He went on to say, "Wherefore the law *is* holy, and the commandment holy, and just, and good" (Rom. 7:12). It looks like Paul, writing under the inspiration of the Holy Spirit, is saying the Law is very much alive and well, doesn't it? Jesus said:

> "Think not that I am come to destroy the Law or the prophets; I am not come to destroy, but to fulfil. For verily I say unto you, Till heaven and earth pass, one jot or one tittle shall in no wise pass from the Law, till all be fulfilled. Whosoever therefore shall break one of these least Commandments and shall teach men so, he shall be called the least in the Kingdom of Heaven, but whosoever shall do and teach them, the same shall be called great in the Kingdom of Heaven" (Mt. 5:17-19).

If fulfill means the same as destroy, then Jesus contradicted Himself in the same sentence, didn't He? Could the love commandments be a summary of the Ten Commandment Law? Could the first love commandment be a summary of the first four Commandments, and the second be a summary of the last six? Also, let's see how God defines love:

➢ "If ye love Me, keep My Commandments" (John 14:15).

➢ "He that hath My Commandments and keepeth them, he it is that loveth Me, and he that loveth Me shall be loved of My Father, and I will love him and will manifest Myself to him" (John 14:21).

➢ "By this we know that we love the children of God when we love God and keep His Commandments.

For this is the love of God: that we keep His
Commandments, and His Commandments are not
grievous" (1 John 5:2,3).

➢ "And this is love: that we walk after His [the
Father's] Commandments" (2 John 1:6).

Are we able to obey God's Law?

It looks like God is defining love as keeping His Ten
Commandment Law, doesn't it? Notice also that He says keeping
His Commandments is not grievous. Most unredeemed people
protest that no one can keep the Ten Commandment Law. It seems
they disagree with God, doesn't it? Is it reasonable to believe God
would give us Ten Commandments, knowing we cannot obey them,
and then tell us that if we do not obey them He will kill us? That
does not sound like the God who reveals Himself in the pages of
Scripture, does it? He goes on to explain why His Commandments
are not grievous: "For whatsoever is born of God overcometh the
world, and this is the victory that overcometh the world; even our
faith" (1 John 5:4).

Even though it is true that ". . . the carnal mind is enmity
against God, for it is not subject to the Law of God, neither
indeed can be" (Rom. 8:7), it is also true that "I can do all things
through Christ which strengtheneth me" (Phlp. 4:13). Do you
suppose "all things" could include His Ten Commandment Law?
What then shall we conclude? I believe all this is telling us that
since God Himself is love (1 John 4:8), then the foundation for
everything is love, including His Ten Commandment Law. In His
love for us He has given us a short list of things we are to avoid
doing (which includes the commandment to honor our parents,
which is a positive way of saying not to dishonor them). If He
had detailed everything we are allowed to do, the list would just
about be infinite, wouldn't it? We are being told that the way we
are to express the two love commandments is by obeying the Ten
Commandment Law (1 John 5:2,3; 2 John 1:6). It may be helpful
to picture the two greatest love commandments as two arms, and
the Ten Commandments as the fingers on the end of those arms.

Why do I focus on just one of the Ten Commandments—the Sabbath? God says we must obey them all, and if we disobey just one, we are transgressors of the Law (Jas. 2:10). It seems to me that the Sabbath commandment is the one that is universally disobeyed, even by Sabbatarians who know it must be obeyed but do not obey it God's way. If God commands us to do something, and tells us how He wants it done and we proceed to obey Him our way instead of His, we aren't really obeying Him, are we? We are replacing our will for His will, which has been our problem from the beginning. Does this sound too extreme? Think it through. Even though salvation is a gift it is not given unless we repent of breaking God's Ten Commandment Law (Acts 2:38). That means obeying them God's way not ours. Christ cannot be our Savior until He is our LORD. This means we must submit to Him as our LORD in repentance and obedience to His Ten Commandment Law.

Will any day do?

Occasionally someone will claim the Bible does not teach that we should keep holy any particular day, only that we observe one day out of six. This seems to me to be so totally at odds with what God commands that it hardly deserves a reply. Nevertheless, (sigh) let's review what God said:

> "And on the seventh day God ended His work which He had made; and He rested on the seventh day from all His work which He had made. And God blessed the seventh day, and sanctified it because that in it He had rested from all His work which God created and made" (Gen. 2:2,3).

God did not rest on *any* day, but the seventh day, *after* six days of creation. Not only that, He blessed that day, and sanctified it. The Sabbath day is the seventh day of the week. That twenty-four hour day is holy time. In the Ten Commandment Law God repeats this fact: "For in six days the LORD made heaven and earth, the sea, and all that in them is, and rested the seventh day. Wherefore the LORD blessed the Sabbath day, and hallowed it" (Ex. 20:11). Also remember that for forty years in the wilderness God gave the Hebrews manna every day except the seventh day—the Sabbath day. How anyone can conclude any day will do in spite of all God says here and elsewhere throughout Scripture is beyond my ability to understand. I guess this is just another example of our ability to see only what we want to see despite the facts.

Has time been lost?

Another excuse I hear for not obeying God's Sabbath Commandment is that time has been lost and no one knows when the original seventh day of creation is. These same people claim they do know when Sunday, the first day of the week is. In a seven-day week, if we know when the first day is, surly we know when the seventh day is, don't we? (Perhaps this is an example of a joke I recently heard: There are three kinds of people in the world; those who can count, and those who can't!). Also Jesus kept the Sabbath day holy. Surly He knew He kept the right day, didn't He? After all, it was He who created the Sabbath day. In the wilderness, the Hebrews received manna from Heaven every day—except on the Sabbath day—for forty years. On the sixth day, they received a double portion, which lasted them over the Sabbath day. After forty years, there was no doubt which day was the Sabbath day. To this day, Jews all over the world keep the Sabbath day holy, and they all know which day it is.

But hasn't the calendar been changed? Yes, it has. Let's take a look at that change and see what affect it had on the Sabbath day. In 45 B.C., during the reign of Julius Caesar, the Julian calendar was created and was used until A.D. 1582 when it was discovered the calendar had an annual error of 12 minutes and 14 seconds, which, over the centuries caused it to be off by ten days. In the *Catholic Encyclopedia*, Vol. 3, p. 740, article "Chronology" we find:

> "It is to be noted that in the Christian period, the order of days in the week has never been interrupted. Thus, when Gregory XIII reformed the calendar in

1582, Thursday, 4 October was followed by Friday, 15 October. So in England, in 1752, Wednesday, 2 September, was followed by Thursday, 14 September."

England was a little slow in making the correction but the result was the same: the sequence of days remained undisturbed.

Lost believers

Toward the end of the Sermon on the Mount, Jesus said:

> "Not every one that saith unto Me, Lord, Lord, shall enter into the Kingdom of Heaven, but he that doeth the will of My Father which is in heaven. Many will say to Me in that day, Lord, Lord, have we not prophesied in Thy name, and in Thy name have cast out devils, and in Thy name done many wonderful works? And then will I profess unto them, I never knew you! Depart from Me, ye that work iniquity" (Mt. 7:21-23).

It seems to me that this statement by Jesus, coming at the end of His Sermon on the Mount is a concise and profound summery of just what we must do to receive eternal life with Him in the Kingdom of Heaven. In verse 21 He tells us that believing in Him is not sufficient. After all, if people call Him Lord they must believe in Him. People who do not believe in Him are not going to call Him Lord, are they? He is saying that even believers will not enter the Kingdom of Heaven if they do not do His Father's will.

The question is what is His Father's will in this context? God's will is expressed in many ways. What specific way is Jesus referring to here? He answers this in verses 22 and 23. These believers are bragging about all the good works they have done in His name—prophesying, casting out demons, and performing many miracles. Then Jesus tells them He never knew them and He orders them to depart from Him. Why? Because they "work iniquity." This means they are practicing lawlessness! So the expression of His Father's will that He is talking about here is His Ten Commandment Law.

There are many who claim that since Jesus told these people, "I never knew you," that means they weren't really believers. If that is true, then Jesus made a false statement because He said these people called Him Lord, a title only believers will use. Paul tells us that "...no man can say that Jesus is the Lord, but by the Holy Ghost" (1 Cor. 12:3). Unbelievers do not have the Holy Spirit, do they? They also did many good works in His name, which is something unbelievers will not do. When He said He never knew them, I believe it was in the sense that He did not have an intimate, loving relation with them because they did not obey His Father's Ten Commandment Law. After all, Jesus is God our creator and He knows everyone better than they know themselves, doesn't He?

Salvation by faith, works, or...

One of the most popular beliefs about salvation is that we don't have to do anything to be saved because salvation is free. If we try to do anything we are neutralizing the gift of salvation. If this belief is true then it seems to me everyone is saved from the moment of his conception in his mother's womb, and nothing we think, say or do will change that fact. Their answer to that is we do have to accept Christ's salvation, or believe He died for our sins, or trust in Him, or something; which contradicts their original statement.

I believe Scripture does teach us that we cannot earn salvation because it is a gift (Eph. 2:8,9). But Scripture also teaches that before we can receive that gift we must meet God's condition, which is to repent of our sins, submit to Jesus Christ as LORD and obey His Ten Commandment Law (Acts 2:38; 3:19; Mt. 7:21-23; 19:17; Heb. 5:9; Rom. 10:3; Jas. 4:7). After writing at length about how we do not earn salvation by our works, Paul, probably anticipating being charged with being against obeying the Ten Commandments, wrote: "Do we then make void the Law through faith? God forbid! Yea, we establish the Law" (Rom. 3:31).

I have been accused of trying to work my way into heaven by keeping the Ten Commandments. Which commandment is work? All but one tell us *not* to do something. One tells us to honor our parents. Is honoring our parents work? The Sabbath commandment specifically tells us *not* to work, and yet this is the one universally ignored. In Ephesians 2:8,9 we are told; "For by grace are ye saved through faith, and that not of yourselves; it is the gift of God, not of works, lest any man should boast." I don't deny that we cannot earn salvation by our works. They usually fail to quote verse 10 though: "For we are His workmanship, created in Christ Jesus unto good works, which God hath before ordained that we should walk in them."

Suppose my rich uncle says he will give me $1,000,000 if I will quit smoking. I am not earning that money, it is a gift if I meet the condition and stop smoking. In the same way we do not *earn* salvation by meeting God's condition for eternal life by repenting of our sins, submitting to Him as LORD and obeying His Ten Commandment Law (Mt. 19:17; 7:21-23). God's condition for salvation is repentance: "For godly sorrow worketh repentance to salvation..." (2 Corinthians 7:10). Jesus warns, "...except ye repent, ye shall all likewise perish" (Lk. 13:3,5).

Unless we have the Spirit of Christ we do not belong to Him (Rom. 8:9). If we do not belong to Christ we are not Christians, are we? The way we receive the Spirit of Christ is to "Repent, and be baptized every one of you in the name of Jesus Christ for the remission of sins and ye shall receive the gift of the Holy Ghost" (Acts 2:38). The context of Romans 8:9 reveals that the "Spirit of Christ" is the Holy Spirit (Ghost).

All through Scripture, those who repent of their sins, submit to Christ/God as LORD and obey His Ten Commandment Law are called Saints. For example:

> ➤ "For the LORD loveth judgment and forsaketh not His saints. They are preserved for ever but the seed of the wicked shall be cut off" (Ps. 37:28).

> ➤ "God is greatly to be feared in the assembly of the saints and to be had in reverence of all them that are about Him" (Ps. 89:7).

> ➤ "Ye that love the LORD, hate evil. He preserveth the souls of His saints. He delivereth them out of the hand of the wicked" (Ps. 97:10).

> ➤ "But the saints of the most High shall take the Kingdom and possess the Kingdom for ever; even for ever and ever" (Dan. 7:18).

> ➤ "Then Ananias answered, Lord, I have heard by many of this man, how much evil he hath done to Thy saints at Jerusalem" (Acts 9:13).

> ➤ "To all that be in Rome, beloved of God, called to be saints . . ." (Rom. 1:7).

In Revelation where everything is coming to a conclusion, and God is wrapping everything up in preparation for the establishment of His Kingdom of Heaven on the earth, we find a couple of interesting verses:

> ➤ "And the dragon was wroth with the woman and went to make war with the remnant of her seed, which keep the Commandments of God and have the testimony of Jesus Christ" (Rev. 12:17).

> ➤ "Here is the patience of the saints; here are they that keep the Commandments of God and the faith of Jesus" (Rev. 14:12).

These two verses in the last book of the Bible define Christians as those who keep the Commandments of God and submit to Jesus as their LORD. This also applies to those saints in the Old Testament since Jesus is the God of the Old Testament. But, some may ask, when did the saints of the Old Testament submit to Jesus as their LORD since Jesus doesn't appear until the New Testament? Good question. Jesus is the God of the Old Testament, therefore the saints who submitted to the God of the Old Testament were in fact submitting to Jesus.

"The conclusion, when all has been heard, is: Fear God, and keep His Commandments, for this is the whole duty of man" (Ecc. 12:13).

CHAPTER THIRTEEN

ARE YOU REALLY A CHRISTIAN?

> ➤ Not every one who says to Jesus, "Lord, Lord," shall enter the kingdom of heaven; but those who do the will of His Father in heaven. Many will say to Him, "Lord, Lord, have we not prophesied in your name and in your name cast out devils and in your name done many wonderful works?" And then He will profess to them, "I never knew you: depart from me, you who practice lawlessness (Mt. 7:21-23).

> ➤ People honor Jesus with their lips, but their hearts are far from Him (Mk. 7:6).

> ➤ They worship Him in vain, teaching for doctrine men's rules (Mk. 7:7).

> ➤ And exchanging His Ten Commandment Law for men's traditions (Mk. 7:8).

> ➤ Resisting sound doctrine to suit their own desires, they gather to themselves many teachers who will say what their itching ears want to hear (2 Tim. 4:3).

> ➤ Turning their ears away from the truth, they embrace myths (2 Tim. 4:4).

> "And just as they did not see fit to acknowledge God any longer, God gave them over to a depraved mind, to do those things which are not proper, being filled with all unrighteousness, wickedness, greed, evil; full of envy, murder, strife, deceit, malice; *they are* gossips, slanderers, haters of God, insolent, arrogant, boastful, inventors of evil, disobedient to parents, without understanding, untrustworthy, unloving, unmerciful; and although they know the ordinance of God, that those who practice such things are worthy of death, they not only do the same, but also give hearty approval to those who practice them" (Rom. 1:28-30 NASB).

> They have a form of godliness, but deny its power, and we should have nothing to do with them (2 Tim. 3:5).

> They are blind guides, and when the blind lead the blind, they all fall into the pit (Mt. 15:14).

> For there is a way that seems right but ends in death (Pr. 14:12; 16:25).

> And nearly everyone is going that way (Mt. 7:13).

> For the whole world is deceived (Rev. 12:9).

> Except the elect (Mt. 24:24).

> But those who would enter eternal life must obey all ten of His Commandments (Mt. 19:17).

> For it we disobey just one Commandment, we are lawbreakers and therefore sinners (Jas. 2:10).

> For sin is the transgression of His Ten Commandment Law (1 John 3:4).

> And the wages of sin is death, but the gift of God is eternal life through Jesus Christ, our Lord as well as our Savior (Rom. 6:23).

> For God so loved the world that He gave His only begotten Son, that whoever believes in Him shall not perish but have everlasting life (John 3:16).

> And Christ is the resurrection and the life, and everyone who believes in Him will receive everlasting life (John 11:25).

> If they obey Him (John 3:36 NASB).

> For if we will repent (and be baptized) in the name of Jesus Christ for the forgiveness of our sins, His Heavenly Father will forgive us and give us the gift of the Holy Spirit (Acts 2:38).

> And unless we have the Spirit of Christ, we do not belong to Him—and we are not Christians (Rom. 8:9).

> And therefore we remain unredeemed sinners—and lost (Rom. 3:23).

> We must repent or perish (Lk. 13:3,5).

> And God is not willing that any should perish, but that all should repent (2 Pet. 3:9).

> And every Christian does repent continually for the forgiveness of his sins, in the name of Jesus Christ, our Lord as well as our Savior (1 John 1:9).

> And obeys all ten of His Commandments, and remains faithful to Him (Rev. 12:17; 14:12).

> ➤ Therefore, there is now no condemnation for those who are in Christ Jesus, our Lord as well as our Savior (Rom. 8:1).

> ➤ If they obey Him (Heb. 5:9)

INDEX

H

T

U
